THE LIBRARY OF POLITICAL ECONOMY

POLITICAL ECONOMY is the old name for economics. In the hands of the great classical economists, particularly Smith, Ricardo and Marx, economics was the study of the working and development of the economic system in which men and women lived. Its practitioners were driven by a desire to describe, to explain and to evaluate what they saw around them. No sharp distinction was drawn between economic analysis and economic policy nor between economic behaviour and its interaction with the technical, social and political framework.

The Library of Political Economy has been established to provide widely based explanations of economic behaviour in contemporary society.

In examining the way in which new patterns of social organization and behaviour influence the economic system and policies for combating problems associated with growth, inflation, poverty and the distribution of wealth, contributors stress the link between politics and economics and the importance of institutions in policy formation.

This 'open-ended' approach to economics implies that there are few laws that can be held to with certainty and, by the same token, there is no generally established body of theory to be applied in all circumstances. Instead economics as presented in this library provides a way of ordering events which has constantly to be updated and modified as new situations develop. This, we believe, is its interest and its challenge.

Editorial Board

Lord Balogh, University of Oxford
Andrew Graham, University of Oxford
Keith Griffin, University of Oxford
Geoffrey Harcourt, University of Cambridge
Roger Opie, University of Oxford
Hugh Stretton, University of Adelaide
Lester Thurow, Massachusetts Institute of Technology

Volumes in the Library

Dangerous Currents: The State of Economics — Lester Thurow
The Political Economy of Nationalism — Dudley Seers
Women's Claims: A Study in Political Economy — Lisa Peattie and Martin Rein
Urban Inequalities under State Socialism — Ivan Szelenyi
Social Innovation and the Division of Labour — Jonathan Gershuny

Women's Claims

*A Study in
Political Economy*

Lisa Peattie & Martin Rein

Oxford University Press
1983

Oxford University Press, Walton Street, Oxford OX2 6DP
London Glasgow New York Toronto
Delhi Bombay Calcutta Madras Karachi
Kuala Lumpur Singapore Hong Kong Tokyo
Nairobi Dar es Salaam Cape Town
Melbourne Auckland
and associated companies in
Beirut Berlin Ibadan Mexico City Nicosia

Oxford is a trade mark of Oxford University Press

Published in the United States
by Oxford University Press, New York

© Lisa Peattie and Martin Rein 1983

All rights reserved. No part of this publication may be reproduced, stored in a retrieval system, or transmitted, in any form or by any means, electronic, mechanical, photocopying, recording, or otherwise, without the prior permission of Oxford University Press

British Library Cataloguing in Publication Data
Peattie, Lisa
Women's claims. — (The Library of political economy)
1. Women — Economic conditions
I. Title   II. Rein, Martin   III. Series
330.9'0088042   HQ1381
ISBN 0-19-877179-7
ISBN 0-19-877180-0 Pbk

Set by Hope Services, Abingdon
Printed in Great Britain
at the University Press, Oxford
by Eric Buckley
Printer to the University

Preface

This book is an attempt to develop a language of political economy which we are calling a theory of claims, via an exploration of the situation of women.

This enterprise emerged, by a somewhat circuitous route, from a project financed by the Ford Foundation to look at economic dualism in industrial and industrializing countries. In this project we were joined by two of our colleagues at MIT, Suzanne Berger and Michael Piore. Berger and Piore have published a book[1] which uses both US and European material to develop an analysis of the politics of economic segmentation. The argument is that in any industrial society powerful groups will find institutionalized means – the specific form of which may vary – to reduce uncertainty for those at the top. The two major strategies for doing this, which in their outcomes in part overlap, are (1) to maintain a tier of small firms – sometimes called the 'informal' or 'traditional' sector – which either directly or indirectly deal with the fluctuating part of demand, and (2) to differentiate a 'secondary labour force' with minimal job security and usually lower pay from established 'primary workers'. There are both political and economic forces at work in the creation of these arrangements, the result of which is a politicized economy characterized by patterns of social and economic segmentation. Discontinuous groups are created, each responsive to distinct, institutionally-defined conditions, and thus each leading its members to distinctive practices and rules of operation which reinforce the segmentation and legitimize the social and legal conventions which structure it.

We were not in disagreement with this analysis, but there were a number of phenomena in which we had become interested which were not captured by the concept of economic dualism, or even by a conceptualization of broad segments.

In Bogota, where Peattie was interviewing people who, looked at in a dualistic framework, would have been described as examples of the 'informal' or 'marginal' sector — keepers of small shops, craftsmen and manufacturers with less than ten employees, street vendors — it became apparent that the economic structure and the economic struggle was not adequately defined, for such people, by the usual interpretation of exclusion from the modern or primary sector. There was an element of alternative, of choice, and of overlap. It was a world of wholesalers and retailers, turfs and territories, which linked persons at the bottom with those at the top in various subsectors having certain shared interests. It was a set of shelters and career lines which constituted alternatives — usually riskier but sometimes with chance for a greater pay-off — to those in the modern firms. In addition, women, especially, organized their economic life in terms of personal attachments which constituted economic opportunities, responsibilities, and risks as well as affectional ones. This was not captured by the language of conventional economics; but neither was it captured by the concept of dualism.[2]

Meanwhile, Rein, looking at the interaction between the work system and the welfare system in the history of low-income families, came to the realization that to such families work and welfare did not constitute the dichotomous categories which seemed the self-evident framework of understanding for policy analysts. For households involved in a perpetually problematic process of income-packaging, work, welfare, and family ties were both alternative supplemental sources of support. His study found not broad segments but a range of economic and social shelters, not alternatives, but overlapping options. The term 'packaging' was intended to describe a clustering of shelters in the area of income.[3]

We began to struggle to develop a language which would capture these phenomena, and developed the theory of claims which is the framework of this book.

In part this enterprise constitutes a criticism of conventional economics. Conventional economics tries to describe the distribution of economic resources 'as if' it followed invariant laws; modelling the operation of these laws, economists hope, will make it possible to predict future economic behaviour. We are taking the view that the primary pattern of distribution is to be understood not as following invariant laws, but as following particular institutional processes. We see the primary pattern as the outcome of a social process of claims in which institutions have historically accommodated to internal and external pressures.

We are also trying to develop a language which makes it possible to make the connection between our understanding of political and social processes at the micro level, in which there is a social negotiation of reality, and the more macrosocial and political economy. People who work in the micro tradition talk about the negotiation of reality between doctor and patient, citizen and bureaucrat, husband and wife; there is a tendency to leave this account at the interpersonal level. Those working at the macro level try to give accounts of broader institutional processes, which tend to be bereft of the personal content of role and experience. We want a language which draws together these different realms of discourse. We hope in this way to contribute to a sharper understanding of process, as well as to help to develop a politics which is meaningful at the level of personal experience.

We believe that the vocabulary of claims provides a research agenda which simultaneously makes it possible to examine the structure of claims at a societal level — the outcomes which are to be accounted for — and the process of claiming by which these outcomes have come about. We seek to integrate structure and process by attempting to describe how things are in society, how things change in society, and who are the direct and indirect agents of these changes.

We pick up pieces of a number of fields of theory, in particular, theory of social movements, without making any attempt to deal with the theory as a whole.

The topic of women was chosen for its convenience as a way of exploring theory. Women seemed to be the obvious topic because, as we began to write, women were making notable claims in all three of the claiming realms we had identified — against the State, in its various roles as regulator, provider, and employer; within the family, with respect to the balance of power, and the allocation of work responsibilities; in the world of work, with respect to the employment policies of the firm.

The topic of women, we have said, we chose for its obvious

convenience. But the choice shaped our thinking. Neither of us thought of ourselves as feminists, but we believe that our perspective may have evolved in a feminist direction in the course of the exploration. More interesting, perhaps, was our realization, at the very end of our writing, that starting with women had led us to a theoretical approach much less centred almost exclusively on work than is characteristic of the political-economy tradition. We came to see both the identification of claiming with economic demands; and the understanding of the claiming process as grounded predominantly in the position of persons and groups in the structure of production; as itself part of the implicit set of conventional understandings which we discuss as the natural.

Since the topic of women was, to us, secondary to the theoretical interest, we did not feel it necessary to bound it carefully. We have discussed mainly the issues of women in the United States in the present, although in some places we have been comparative and in others historical.

We owe a debt to two different groups of people. The first are those who helped us to hammer out our thoughts on claims: Suzanne Berger, Michael Piore, John Harris, Lee Rainwater, and Hugh Stretton especially.

On the application of this framework to the situation of women, we owe a special debt to Lance Liebman, Professor in the Harvard Law School, who helped us in understanding the legal framework of claims, in conceptualizing claiming more generally, and in locating citations to specific issues against which we could test our analysis.

Carole Joffe greatly deepened our understanding of the issues surrounding abortion, and sensitized us to issues in the women's movement.

Gary Marx helped us to think about social movements in general.

Valerie Nelson helped us to specific examples of the politics of women's claiming.

Robert Weiss did not work with us on any single particular issue but was a continuing sounding-board for our ideas and a source of insight and stimulation about women in society.

Frances Fox Piven, Robert Fogelson, and Hedy Rudolph gave helpful criticism, both general and detailed, on a preliminary draft.

Other people who helped us with the women's issues were: Helen Hughes, Dorothy Klubock, Sara, Julia, and Miranda Peattie, Mary Belenky, Sylvia Vaterlaus, Jennifer Schirmer, and Yasmine Ergas.

We owe a special thanks to Barbara Wiget for the enormous help she provided in disentangling the complex maze of definitions and statistics in the discussion of women and the State. She helped set the statistical foundation for a much larger comparative study of the State as employer.

NOTES

[1] Suzanne Berger and Michael Piore, *Dualism and Discontinuity in Industrial Societies*, Cambridge, NY: Cambridge University Press, 1980.
[2] Lisa R. Peattie, 'Anthropological Perspectives on the Concepts of Dualism, the Informal Sector, and Marginality in Developing Urban Economies', *International Regional Science Review*, Vol. 5, No. 1, pp. 1-31, 1980.
[3] Martin Rein and Lee Rainwater, 'Patterns of Welfare Use', *Social Service Review*, December 1978, pp. 511-34, and Martin Rein, *From Policy to Practice*, NY: M.E. Sharpe Inc., 1983.

Contents

1. THE IDEA OF THE NATURAL   1
2. CLAIMS, CLAIMING, AND CLAIM STRUCTURES   16
3. HOUSEWORK: WOMEN IN THE DOMESTIC ECONOMY   37
4. WOMEN AND WORK: THE INCOMPLETE REVOLUTION   59
5. WOMEN AND THE STATE   80
6. THE WOMEN'S MOVEMENT AS A PROCESS OF CLAIMING   102

EPILOGUE   127

INDEX   137

CHAPTER 1

The Idea of the Natural

EVERY movement for social reform comes up, sooner or later, against the barrier of the natural: that which cannot be changed because it is in the order of things, outside the span of intervention. We may argue about the specific wage differential between janitors and professors, but it is typically regarded as only natural that professors should receive substantially higher wages than janitors, because professors' skills are in shorter supply, their acquisition requires a much longer investment in training, and their contribution to society is greater. We may argue about the circumstances under which it is appropriate for women to work, and the kinds of employment which they may appropriately enter, and we may argue about the proper allocation of rights and responsibilities between husband and wife in the family, but most people consider it is only natural that the man should be both the main breadwinner and the family head because women naturally are best adapted to rearing children and men are able to earn better in the world of work outside.

While both these examples deal with the division of labour and the division of reward, what they share more crucially for our purposes is the constraint imposed on negotiation and argument by the idea of the natural. This idea recurs in many specific realms where roles and resources are apportioned. In any such realm renegotiation of resources will touch on the boundary, and produce arguments as to how far deliberate intervention can change the natural order of things. In this essay we propose to use examples from several areas in order to focus attention on the idea of the natural itself. We intend to develop a framework for social analysis and criticism which overrides the dichotomy between the natural and artificial. We treat that which is ordinarily identified as the natural – 'economic processes' and 'culture' – as the working-out of institutions, and that which we identify as 'policy' as a natural societal process. We then intend to develop an alternative vocabulary which we call a theory of claims, which would make it easier to treat as the central topic the processes by which the line between the natural and the artificial, seen now as perpetually being negotiated, is drawn. Our interest is both practical and theoretical. Epistemologically we want to show that the concepts which we use to describe social reality are always a function of our social purposes: and that the conceptualization of a natural realm contrasted to an artificial one is itself a purpose-serving social construction. Practically, we hope through this discussion to open up for political argument and activity, areas traditionally closed off by the line drawn between artificial and natural.

We can formulate this insight in more general terms. When we think about society, we make an implicit distinction between the rules and institutions which are ours to make and remake and the aspects of society which are given, which constitute the context, the parameters, and the constraints on our action. We may call this way of thinking a form of thought which distinguishes the 'artificial' from the 'natural'.[1] Both aspects of society are, of course, man-made. This is understood. But we think about the two sets of institutions and processes differently. Some things appear to us as 'given'. The historian may tell us that institutions which now appear as part of the order of nature came into existence through political argument and deliberate intervention, and that the institutions of deliberate policy-making which we now possess came into being as part of great social movements which it is possible to think of sociologically as natural. But as things stand at one point in time we make an implicit distinction between an 'artificial' realm of intervention and policy and the rest of society — naturally given — which we may modify, compensate for, adjust to.

That which is natural may be so in more than one way. The various ways of being natural have differing sorts of standing and varying levels of necessity. Some things appear to us to be natural because of appropriateness; surely if you tried to do it differently, you would feel so peculiar or out of place that no one in their right mind would care to; a woman would not want to attend a stag party. Some things appear natural because the system requires them; everything would fall apart if we changed; children should have a mother to care for them. Still other things appear natural in the sense of being the only possibility; people would be incapable of doing it differently; a woman isn't strong enough to do certain jobs.

Logically, it would seem that these various ways of being natural represent differing levels of inevitability and therefore, as they attach to particular issues, give these issues differing degrees of standing on a particular historical agenda for change. But things seem to be more complex. We may see these various kinds of rationales applied to a particular issue, and that while we may suppose a priori that appropriateness would yield before system-requiredness and system-requiredness before capacity, this is not necessarily what happens.

When during the war it was decided that it was necessary to attract women into heavy industrial work such as welding, it was necessary first to counter the belief that women might be incapable of doing this sort of work. When women were trained to weld, there appeared the problem of the inappropriateness of introducing women into a masculine world of macho behaviour and bad language. At the end of the war, when it appeared necessary to have women withdraw from the industrial work-force to make way for men, the argument was from system-requiredness; it was critically important for women to be free to play the role of wives and mothers.

The distinction between natural and artificial is basic to policy research, to political argument, and to social-scientific analysis, as it constitutes an implicit element in the conceptual definition of the fields. Social science deals with the way things are in the realm of the natural. Politics argues about what should be done within the realm of the artificial. Policy analysis deals with what can rationally be done given the purposes defined by the political process.

Institutions in the realm of the natural have a sort of special legitimacy as that well-enough which might as well be let alone. But intervention in the realm of the artificial has a kind of special status also. Enquiry into these activities of intervention in the framework of policy analysis, decision-making, and programme design permits us to think about intervention and intervenors apart from the sort of examination of origins, interests, and motives to which we subject institutions in the realm of the natural. The technocratic approach as a social construction, and the boundary between natural and artificial as an aspect of this approach, is thus an important aspect of the political and social equilibrium which at any given time in a given society makes it possible to do some things and not others.

Since there is evidently no use arguing about what should be done about things which are beyond our control, which are properly understood as part of the natural order, the boundary between natural and artificial is important in setting off the area for political argument and policy analysis from that of the order of nature which must be understood. This line of course may be, and is, set differently in different societies and in different periods. The socialist-command economies place the realm of economic institutions squarely within the realm of the artificial, whereas the free-market societies, while intervening in the economic, still consider such interventions as being marginal modifications of the natural. The Cuban concept of creating a 'New Man' took human nature as malleable, and as part of the artificial; most societies, including socialist ones, see a natural realm of the personal, familial, and traditional which lies outside the reach of policy.

Nevertheless, even in the democratic capitalist societies the boundary between the natural and the artificial is not settled but continually being renegotiated. In particular, we argue and conduct research around the issue of whether a given phenomenon is properly placed on one side or the other of the boundary. We argue, for example, whether the natural intelligence of working-class children can be substantially modified by lead-paint prohibitions or early childhood education, two different ways of organizing artificial interventions into the world of the natural. More generally, the analytic conventions of economics are in search of models of phenomena treated as natural ones. In contrast political economy points to the role of social and political institutions in shaping economic outcomes. Thus political economy is, in effect, either arguing for some actual shift in the position of the boundary between natural and artificial, or — which may be just as important — drawing attention to the fact that this boundary is, in principle, shiftable.

The ways in which we conceptualize the natural are themselves derived from our experience and programmatic interests in the sphere of the artificial. Therefore, new social movements and newly organized interests will tend to shift the boundary between the natural and the artificial.

Since the setting of the boundary between the natural and the artificial is a part of the struggle of interests, ideas about the nature of reality and the boundary between the natural and the artificial are both the product of and a weapon of struggle. At any given time, the institutions available for action shape ideas of the possible, and hence of the boundary between the natural and the artificial. On the other hand, ideas of the natural shape organization. Action and politics shape ideas. The organization of interests presses new conceptions of reality. But ideas shape action, as conceptions about the natural and artificial dominate our theory and the scope and character of intervention.

We will develop two examples of the resetting of the boundary between the natural and the artificial. The first is in our thinking about poverty and indigence. The second is our view of women and their place in society.

Views of Poverty

If we open our poverty story in England at the end of the eighteenth century, we see that poverty — certainly an issue for discussion, particularly in years of agricultural scarcity — was being discussed in a framework which made little or no distinction between a realm of market forces and one of deliberate intervention. This was natural enough, given that the setting for discussion was rural parishes dominated by a landowning élite who both as employers and as ratepayers and as the managers of the parish-relief structure had all the ways of coping with poverty in their own hands. It was natural, then, to make little distinction between one sort of institution and another; in effect, wages and relief from the rates and private charity were all part of a single set of rural social institutions.

Employers . . . did not regard wage rates as fixed by automatic economic laws, but rather by an arbitrary assessment of what was 'fair' or 'necessary'. Even more important, they did not clearly differentiate between wages and relief: there were reports of a partial reversion to paying wages in kind, farmers providing corn as a direct supplement to the labourer's diet and even where cash wages were increased it was usually as part of a general scheme to meet the demands of scarcity ... Others recommended increasing the number of men employed beyond farmers' immediate needs, especially in winter, to increase the labourer's annual if not daily wage. Relief in money or in kind, from the rates or by private subscription; subsidies on foodstuffs; increased wages or employment: the mingling of such devices might appear untidy or unjust to those who distinguish between economic rights and charity, but most have seemed obviously expedient to meet a crisis expected to be temporary.[2]

Both poverty, as the necessity for most persons to work at near subsistence, and indigence, as the inability of some unlucky or improvident individuals to gain their subsistence, appeared as part of the natural order of things. One could not have thought of eliminating poverty, although charity could relieve indigence.

The notion of poverty as 'natural' as an intellectual construction is the creation of Malthus in very large part. Intellectual construction it surely was, for part of Malthus's invention was to argue not from an examination of particular processes and institutions, but from a deductive analysis of the relationship between population and resources. Malthus described a system of natural forces into which any intervention was likely to prove mischievous and counter-productive. Except under rather exceptional circumstances, relief of poverty would, it was argued, naturally lead to a press of population on resources which would in the long run simply accentuate the poverty and want it had been intended to alleviate.

The Malthusian analysis came to constitute the established framework for policy discussion. However, since in practice few people — including Malthus — were prepared to simply let people starve, programmes for coping with poverty continued to be brought forward. Intellectually, these had to engage with the new conception of the natural. Thus argument over the Poor Law came to be progressively coloured by Malthusian ideas. Those who argued for limiting intervention found Malthusian ideas a ready basis; but those who sought to do something to relieve hardship equally felt called upon to develop proposals which could be justified as provoking minimal disturbance in the natural order. In the Poor Law reforms, this strategy of minimizing disturbance found its key in Bentham's invention of less eligibility, which proposed to leave the market undisturbed by ensuring that any form of public relief would provide a standard below that of the wage-worker.

In looking at this period, however, we see that the invention of the natural did not immediately give rise to its opposite — the invention of the artificial. Instead, the 'natural' state of affairs was contrasted to a set of interventions which were simply thought of as unnatural. These interventions were not yet considered justified by standing managerially above and outside society. They did not yet constitute a realm of the artificial. It took a hundred years of institutional experimentation with various kinds of intervention to cope with poverty and destitution, and the sense of consensus produced by a great war, to produce that realm of the artificial which we now identify as the welfare state.

The welfare state implies a different conception of intervention than that of reluctant charity programmes inspired by a conflict between charity and common sense. We now have the idea of 'policy', which takes some aspect of the natural order (wages, unemployment, incomes, fertility) and treats it as something which intervention can cause to be treated differently in the natural world. The idea that there is a legitimate realm of the artificial becomes completed when a special class of policy analysts is conceived, and these analysts are then located in a separate institutional arrangement. These analysts, paradoxically, thus derive their legitimacy by conceiving themselves as students of the laws of the natural which must be described, generalized, and applied in the field of the man-made initiative of 'policy'.

In the conceptual framework utilized by these policy analysts the natural is subdivided into two: the realm of economics and the realm of the social. The economic is the realm of rational choice and resource distribution. The realm of the social is the lives of people and the primary institution in which they organize their lives, the family. The economic realm is governed by principles of efficiency, rational choice, and maximization. The social realm is governed by concerns for affect, particularism, tradition, reciprocity. The two realms of the natural reinforce each other. The family is used to reproduce and socialize labour used in the economic realm, and the economic realm produces resources used by the social realm. The realm of the artificial or political is the realm of policy choice.

However, that choice is not unconstrained. Deliberate intervention must respect the requirement for efficient functioning in the economic, and it must equally respect the natural rules which perpetuate and maintain the family.

Policy analysis as conventionally understood is believed to consist of grasping the principles which organize each of the two realms of the natural and the character of their interaction, as well as the distinction between the natural and the artificial and the proper interaction between the two.

When our story began, there was not a conception of a natural order separate from a realm of intervention; wages and transfers were intertwined and overlapping aspects of the single rural society. But once there came to be a conception of a natural world obeying its own laws, intervention by contrast became a problem to be considered. In the early nineteenth century the notion was to intervene as little as possible, subject to the constraints imposed by Christian concern for suffering. 'Less eligibility' was the invention for doing this. On the other hand, within the framework of the Welfare State, intervention becomes positively welcomed. But it must still be thought of as needing to adapt itself to, and be limited by, the characteristics of the natural order.

The obvious example of accommodation is that income-transfer programmes must not disrupt work incentives in the economic realm and the organization of family life in the societal realm. Witness the consternation and dismay which follow when welfare is alleged to break up families.

Since the economic realm is assumed to generate all resources to be distributed, its continued integrity has a special position. Above all, the efforts to improve the distribution of income must not damage the incentive to work. Income-reshuffling efforts should be neutral or ideally positive with respect to work incentives.

Note that in these contemporary discussions, as in the earlier discussions of poverty and the Poor Law, it is only the proper mechanisms for dealing with the natural which are under discussion. We think of the primary distribution of income as being an original distribution of income, which implies that it comes about through natural market forces. So long as we have no intention of any continuing intervention in the distribution, it would be uncomfortable and inappropriate to think of it in any other way.

The same set of issues arise when we intervene in the job structure rather than intervening by direct income transfers. In this area, there is a body of concern having to do with equalizing opportunity and with breaking down institutional rigidities inhibiting access to jobs — racial and sexual discrimination. But the efforts to seek an institutional rearrangement of hiring, promotion, compensation, and working conditions must respect the occupational structure generated by a given level of technology and productive system. Again, there is a realm of the natural to which policy must accommodate.

If we turn to trace the role of women through the story of boundary shifts between the natural and the artificial, we will also see as critically important the division, which we have mentioned with respect to thinking about poverty, between two realms of the natural: the economic and the social. The distinction is important to the story of women because women's *primary* social placement on one side of the line between the social and the economic, within the world of the family, has dominated the situation of women; and as the issue of the status of women has come recently to enter the agenda of the artificial as a policy issue, it has done so in a form which reflects the prior and underlying placement of women within the social rather than the economic.

Views of Women

If we start the story of the 'woman question' at the same point we started that of the poverty question, that is, at the end of the eighteenth century, we would find that the separation between the economic and the social is clearly beginning, but not yet dominant.

The institutional reorganization which separated workplace from home-place happened only gradually. Much of early capitalist development involved work on the putting-out system. The capitalist garment manufacturer was not controlling a factory, he was giving out piles of garment pieces to be carried home and sewed, largely by women and children, in the domestic setting. Bakeries and breweries were family firms. As Zaretsky[3] points out, the early stages of capitalism, using the household as the major unit of productive organization, involved a strengthening of and emphasis on the family. The social and the economic were thus a single realm.

As the first factories came into existence, the family, instead of being shut out, was carried into the work-place. Primary workers brought in their own helpers, usually their own children and other relatives. The patterns of commitment and authority within the family were thus carried over intact into the factory setting. With time, however, and partly as a result of legislation restricting the work-hours of children to be fewer than those of adults, the domain of the family and the domain of the factory became separated. Meanwhile as the economy became organized into larger firms, the family as a unit of production ceased to be the norm. Work-place and domestic space became clearly separated. Individuals went out from the family to work, and returned home.

Through the nineteenth century an important source of household monetary income was brought by women working at home through taking in lodgers. In the new industrial cities, the shortage of housing for new entrants and the desire on the part of established residents to shift some of their burden made for a mutually desirable bargain in the renting-out of space to lodgers. The result was an activity situated squarely on the boundary between the economic and the social: using the household dwelling as its fixed capital, utilizing the same technology and skills as the housekeeper used in unpaid domestic work towards the gaining of a monetary income.

That male wages should support the household economy was accepted in principle, but not carried out in practice because the male could not, by his own earnings, command a wage high enough to maintain a family at an adequate standard of well-being. Hence it was necessary to have other members of the family in work. At the turn of the century it was inappropriate for wives to enter the labour market.

Their economic activity was confined to taking in lodgers. However, it was common practice that the sons and daughters worked and pooled their resources to support household economy. It was only after World War I that the male head of the household earned enough to maintain the family on his own earnings. But this did not last very long. By the 1960s, the two-earner family had become increasingly common. Of course, this implied a standard of adequacy which had increased in absolute terms, but the relative amounts needed to get along or to keep out of poverty were surprisingly stable over time in the post-war period.[4] Now, of course, the sons and daughters were by and large in school and it was the wife who went out to work to contribute to the family income. This heralded the participatory revolution in women's work, namely the entry of wives and then later wives who were also mothers into the labour force. (Women who headed families with children always tended to work and their labour-force participation did not change significantly over time.)

By the time it was possible to speak of a developed realm of the artificial, of a set of policy-making institutions rationalized on the principle of expertise, the separation between the economic and the social had been conventionally established for some time. Also established was the principle in which the primary breadwinner was the male, and wives and daughters entered the economic realm as — from the family perspective — secondary contributors. Intervention by 'the artificial' into both firms and family followed a conventional understanding of the natural. In this body of understanding, there is a separation between the economic and the social, a 'natural' relationship between family and economy, and a 'natural' role for women within the family and within the labour force. The placing of the 'economic' outside the family — in a realm of the firm and the monetized — gave wage labour a sharply different social meaning from domestic production. The primary role of males in the economic world of wage labour gave men a dominant position within the family. The combination of women's primary responsibility for unpaid domestic labour and lower earnings in the wage-labour market ensured that women's attachment to the labour force would be intermittent, and that from the perspective of employers women could function as a secondary labour force less demanding with respect to both wages and job security than men.

This view of the nature of things had important consequences for the economic role of women, and for the design of policy shaping women's jobs and earnings.

Australia provides a curious example of active intervention by legal experts within the above-described framework around the turn of the century. An Arbitration Commission was formed to set a basic household wage. Reflecting the conventional acceptance of the 'natural', the judges on the commission defined the earning unit as comprising a male, his wife, and two dependent children. The dependent role of wives is assumed. As wages in predominantly women's occupations were set, it was deemed to be 'natural' that these should be 54 per cent of men's. Only in order to protect the male wage from undercutting by women was it determined that when women worked in predominantly male occupations they should receive the same wage as men.

Although the arbitration mechanism used in Australia never took hold in other industrialized societies, the underlying assumptions are quite general and pervade both policy argument and wage and employment practice. The assumption that women's primary place is in the home, and that men must be the main breadwinners serves to rationalize both occupational differentiation by sex and sharp wage differentials between 'men's jobs' and 'women's jobs', as well as a division of labour within the family in which it is women's 'responsibility' to do housework and rear children and men 'help out'.

Thus when, in the context of the emergence of the women's movement, policy experts came to consider the existing occupational and wage structure as it related to women, the issues were complicated by a body of assumptions as to the 'natural'. It had become established that economic intervention would occur provided that such intervention was done so as to leave the basic 'natural economic processes' intact. If intervention was now to be done with respect to women's issues in the work-place, there was a collision with principles arising out of the 'nature' of the family and of women's place in it.

Thus, when the American Telephone and Telegraph Company was taken into court on charges of discrimination against women in its hiring and promotion policies, it seemed only reasonable for AT&T's lawyers to argue that 'naturally' women had weaker attachment to the job than men, dropping in and out of the labour force as family responsibilities emerged or waned, and that their career aspirations were also naturally weaker. The importance of the case made against AT&T by the Equal Opportunity Commission was precisely to question both the naturalness of women's work behaviour and of the incentives offered to women by AT&T, to which, it was argued, the women's behaviour was a response.[5]

Conventional understanding of the nature of the natural also shaped the design of policy in the realm of the social, i.e. family. Here we are dealing with an implicit understanding of the natural division of labour where the two-parent family is viewed as the critical institution for rearing children and within that family woman held the primary responsibility for mothering — bearing, rearing children — and wiving, providing emotional support to the husband from the alienation he experienced at work and attending to the chores of keeping the house. Parsons summarized this essential task as fulfilling the 'expressive' role. Mothering and wiving are thought to represent a single, inextricable natural role.

When the realm of the artificial enters the situation defined in this way, it does so in the form of specific programmes and policies such as day care, fertility control, Medicaid for abortion, maternity leave etc. Debate on such programmes and policies takes the form of arguing whether they do or do not 'support the family'; only eccentrics would argue whether supporting the family is a good thing, since 'the family' as given is the natural way for people to live. Issues are confronted somewhat more directly when social agencies are faced with developing policies concerning standards for adoption, or principles of family counselling. In order to regularize decisions in concrete cases, such agencies find themselves discussing principles without being able to arrive at a settled and coherent point of view. Of course, policy becomes implicit in their practice. At present, practice with respect to adoption and custody decisions shows a disposition to redefine the content of the natural family, as we witness shifts in decisions concerning inter-religious, inter-racial, and now single-parent adoptions for women and perhaps even men, and cases in which a homosexual parent may be given custody of a child in a divorce.

This is an account of the evolution of a system of ideas. The ideas with which we now engage the world both in thought and in action seem to involve a separation between 'economic' and 'social' issues, and to set forth a special realm of expert intervention. These distinctions are the conventional wisdom. By describing these distinctions in terms of a boundary between the 'natural' and the 'artificial' we have tried to get at the underlying assumptions which organize our structuring of social reality. We have tried to show that this system of ideas evolved over time, dividing the social from the economic and institutionalizing the role of policy expertise, and that the boundary between natural and artificial as well as the specific content of the natural have shifted.

These general ideas become altered by, used by, and are the consequences of a complicated set of historical processes. We have not dealt with these here. We have only provided a very preliminary sketch of the shifting ideas themselves. Nor have we done more than suggest in a very preliminary way what these ideas mean in social practice — a practice which we believe they both shape and reflect. To do so is to treat society as an arena of argument, in which groups and individuals come to assert interests and to have those interests recognized by others in terms of rationales. In the attempt to develop a vocabulary which treats the interaction between ideas, interests, and action in a single framework, we have elaborated what we call a theory of claims. In the next chapter we attempt to describe this vocabulary, and in subsequent chapters to ground it in specific examples taken from women's issues and the women's movement.

NOTES

[1] The clearest identification of this distinction can be found in Herbert Simon's (1969) *The Sciences of the Artificial*, Cambridge, Mass.: MIT

Press. The virtue of the book is that it makes explicit the tacit framework that organizes enquiry into policy issues. Simon's vocabulary of discourse is that of 'command variables', 'objective functions', 'fixed parameters', 'constraints', and 'inner and outer environments'.

[2] H. R. Poynter, *Society and Pauperism: English Ideas on Poor Relief 1795-1834*, London: Routledge and Kegan Paul, 1969, p. 48.

[3] Eli Zaretsky, *Capitalism, the Family and Personal Life*, NY: Harper and Row, 1976.

[4] Lee Rainwater, *What Money Buys*, New York: Basic Books, 1979.

[5] Phyllis Wallace, *Equal Employment Opportunity and the AT & T Case*, Cambridge, Mass: MIT Press, 1976.

CHAPTER 2

Claims, Claiming, and Claim Structures

Traditional Approaches

HOW shall we understand modern industrial societies? Two general modes of understanding have emerged. One way is represented by the powerful abstractions of formal economic analysis; the other is a more descriptive 'institutional' view which sociologists, anthropologists, and political scientists might employ with respect to the same phenomena.

The division arises in large part out of the sharply different methodologies employed by the different disciplines, but it also has consequences for the boundaries of the subject-matter. Economic analysis centres on individual choices between competing goods. It does not usually inquire into the sources of preference; it further has difficulty in dealing with actions taken out of coercion or commitment. Thus it has serious difficulty with the complex combinations of coercion, commitment, and group belief and value structure which make up human institutions. Because it deals most easily with monetized human activities, in which the ambiguities of transactions have been smoothed over by reduction to price, economic analysis tends to set off as 'the economy' monetized human activities from others. The institutional view, on the other hand, may treat monetary transactions as an aspect of a much larger field of interactions describable under such headings as family and kinship, social institutions, power.

The development of a science of economics, and the delineation of a field of action called 'economic' to which it might refer constitute an element in the history of the development of industrial society itself. As Polanyi points out, before that development of a market economy which he calls 'The Great Transformation'[1] there were not thought to be such things as pure 'economic activities'. Making a living, distribution were embedded in the general institutions and activities of society, and were thought of as aspects of the interplay of specific social groups; this is still the perspective of *The Wealth of Nations*.

Karl Polanyi describes the development of a market economy as the appearance of a new kind of societal organization in which an 'economic sphere' became sharply separated from other institutions in society. But it also had a normative element; it played a role in particular efforts to shape society according to distinctive visions of the proper role of the state in the new order. The conception of a separate 'economic realm' seems, oddly, to have served both Left and Right. On the one hand, the understanding of the 'operation of the market' as the sum of a myriad of transactions between individuals each seeking to maximize his own well-being proposed an adjustment of interests through the Invisible Hand more perfect than any state intervention might possibly achieve, and justified the unrestricted pursuit of self-interest by business firms. On the other hand, for the collectivists, the assertion that the 'market economy' did daily violence to human life served as the rationale for a demand seen as inevitable that, in the modern phrase, 'Politics take Command', and society reasserts its humanizing control over the economic process.

Thus there were many reasons for the conceptualization of society as comprising an 'economic sphere' in contrast to realms of the political and social. It only remained for the marginalists to exploit this vision theoretically, to place economics, the 'Queen of the Sciences', in a dominant position among the social sciences, and to separate its formulations very sharply from the more descriptive and institutional picture of reality arising from sociological and anthropological fieldwork, and also separating 'economics' from 'political economy' and some parts of economic history.

However, certain difficulties arise out of this separation. The first lies in the recognition that within advanced industrial societies there persists a segment of firms (the 'traditional sector') with characteristics different from those toward which the logic of ecnomic efficiency had been thought to be tending, and that such societies continue to utilize, even to import, a body of 'secondary workers', again with the characteristics which one might have imagined that development would have rendered obsolete. 'Economic' explanations of these phenomena, beyond simple lag theory, focus on vicious cycles, and disequalizing feedback mechanisms;[2] but even these 'economic' explanations imply the development of sharp institutional differentiations and even subcultural differences generated by the economic processes and thus lead into theories of society. Furthermore, an alternative mode of explanation looks to the political and social functions served by the perpetuation of the 'traditional sector' or 'secondary workers' and finds in public policy the reason for their existence.[3]

The problem also arises in the attempt to integrate the powerful abstractions of economic theory with the real world of interests and institutions so as to deal effectively with the latter. The gap between the two, present from the beginning of formal marginalist theories, could only intensify as economic entities became larger, the 'market' more and more subject to their management, and the role of government in the economy more extensive. Dense institutional reality and formal models were too far apart for the latter to serve conveniently as the basis for working policy and programme design. One response to this difficulty is to reject the issue. In the words of Frank Knight: 'Economics, in the usual meaning, as a science of principles, is not, primarily, a descriptive science in the empirical sense at all. It "describes" *economic* behaviour and uses the concept to explain the working of our modern economic organization and also to criticize and suggest changes.'[4] For an economist interested in making a contribution to policy formulation or policy criticism this sort of position is not very helpful, and economists in this position generally follow the strategy of trying to incorporate into their models some representation, if only rather schematic, of the characteristics of economic institutions. Theories of wage determination have to take account of labour unions and collective bargaining; theories of inflation have to take account of monopoly and the goals other than profit maximization of the modern firm.

Another way the issue arises is in the attempt to reconcile the ideas of necessity and functionalism which seem to be implied by economic analysis with the evident variability of economic systems. While differences between the economic institutions and managerial forms in various societies are sometimes explained as the residues of differing pre-industrial bases, bound to be further eroded by processes of development seen as inherently convergent, there are contrasting pieces of evidence. The finding that French and German firms producing the same good or service with the same technology consistently do so with strikingly different managerial structures and different skills assortments[5] suggests, for example, that 'industrial society' constitutes not a single type, but rather a series of types. There must therefore be considerable scope for institutional variability across societies characterized by the same economic structure. These difficulties are widely recognized, and one can identify a recently revived interest in Marxism and 'political economy' as arising as much out of an interest in institutional variation as out of the traditional Marxist search for universal laws of change.

We are also struggling with this conceptual problem, and as our approach, have attempted to build a descriptive language around the notion of *claims*.

We use the term claims because we want to call attention to two aspects of what people receive in society. There is an element of right, entitlement, or just deserts; however, these are not always automatically forthcoming, and there is also an active process by which individuals within institutions demand, extract, request, enforce their bids for resources. Groups and individuals continue to press to extend their entitlements, and thus claiming is an ongoing, always incomplete process.[6]

On the other hand, as claims become institutionalized and are no longer contested they come to be embedded in social roles and to appear as part of the natural order — the way people naturally act — or to appear as the consequences for groups and individuals of sensible social policy. We believe that when the entitlement is granted as of right, this must be understood as the outcome of an earlier process of claim-pressing. It is a kind of truce in an ongoing struggle which took the form of requests, bids, bargains, or negotiation. Because there is no sharp line of demarcation in this ongoing process, the terminology is often confusing.

The attempt to develop a vocabulary around the concept of claims was a response to our need for a language to describe political economy at the level of the individual and the household. Our aim in so doing was to explicitly reject the placing of claims from work — called 'earnings' — in a special status as given by economic process, and, in contrast, to develop a language within which 'earnings' may be seen quite as institutionally determined as claims on consumption arising out of kinship relations or through the welfare system. In this way of looking at the world, 'economic' processes are seen as one part of a world of political rules and social conventions. However, as we began to lay out the system of categories arising from the idea of claims, we found that it led us back to the macro level — to the system as a whole. Claims and claiming has an individual aspect, but individual claims are made, necessarily, in terms of social conventions, systems of legal and customary entitlements, collective institutions by which claims are asserted. We found that we wanted to look at claiming as a social and political process, with complex and specific histories in particular societies, and at claim structures as wholes.

This perspective, up to a point that of the Marxists, clearly parts company from them in treating the system of earnings as centrally problematic, rather than as given by the structure of production. It is possible to treat 'work' itself as part of that body of conventions which Polanyi saw as the construction of a new social reality. In this extended view, 'work' is no more self-evidently a claim on consumption than any other; the concepts of 'work' and 'wages' may be seen as social conventions which, rather arbitrarily, put some institutionally determined claims on consumption into a special status.

From this point of view, we would treat 'earnings from work' as one component in an institutionalized system of claims on consumption, along with other sets of claims generated in the kinship system (as in the case of wives, children) or against the state (as in the case of welfare). This indeed seems to be the sort of view which emerges from looking at the way low-income households cope; it is not a question of work versus welfare so much as a problem of assembling, from various sources, what we have come to call packages of income.

Claim packages

A *claim package* is the unique assemblage of claims which a household puts together in attempting to maximize its welfare within a given claim system.[7] This claim package involves, at least at some level, the choice and the selection from a range of possible alternative income sources. In modern industrial societies, individuals and families can derive income from such sources as earnings by a principal wage-earner, earnings by other members of the family, income from assets, income from private retirement plans, income in the form of gifts or recognition of legal obligations (child support) by relatives, and income from a number of public transfer sources.

Welfare reform has to be understood in the context of the other kinds of claims that families are able to make on society for income. One of these, claims from participation in the labour market, has received a great deal of attention in policy research over the past decade on welfare reform. But it is only one of several kinds of income sources.

Claims confer more than income; they also confer position and status. The claims that an individual can reasonably assert are determined by previous position in society. For example, as Charles Reich points out, within the variety of claims against government, some, such as various kinds of licences and mortgage rebates, are available only to persons who already enjoy some measure of social and economic resources.[8] Such claims against the State constitute a way of multiplying the privileges of position. At the other end of the spectrum are claims such as welfare, food stamps, public housing. Thus it appears that claims both confer status and are determined by previous status.

Therefore, the way in which claim packages are put together varies according to choice and to social placement. Different systems provide different possibilities (the variegated street trades of the developing countries in part represent a response to the absence of a 'welfare system' in the American sense); city and rural patterns differ; there are marked regional variations; and there are differences among classes. That variation exists within classes suggests that choice as well as constraints are important — low-income families with the same level of income have quite different packages depending on work–welfare choices, on the husband–wife earning choice, and on headship choices — e.g. willingness to become a female-headed family.

When we look at the distribution of economic resources as depending on the overall structure of society, not merely on the performance of the economy, to what kinds of issues do we direct our attention? These issues may be described as falling into three broad categories: the nature of claims, claiming as a process in which claims evolve over time, and claims structures viewed as the outcomes of this process.

Claim Systems

Industrial societies may be described in terms of three major realms within which claims are generated and honoured: family, economy, government. Each realm provides an avenue for establishing claims. The principles on which claims rest are different in each of these realms. But each realm is also sufficiently differentiated so that within it one finds many principles concurrently operating. Thus, in practice, the principles underlying each of the claims realms become blurred at the margins. Therefore, it is at the margins that the most interesting questions lie, because it is here that we find the possibility for redefinition and change.

The *family* is bound together by the principle of solidarity. Reciprocal obligations within the family derive from the sense of community bound together by blood. The entitlements and the obligations derive from these blood ties. Thus the principles of filial responsibility of a daughter or son to her/his parents differ sharply from the responsibility of spouses for each other. In addition, the established principles for support of a mother or for support of a wife change over time with the growth of other institutional arrangements (such as pensions, nursing home care, etc.).

Marital separation and divorce, and patterns of cohabitation are also redefining the claims of spouses against each other. Of course, the children's claim against the family differs yet again. Perhaps, at one time, children were seen as an investment, in the quite literal sense of providing the child with resources when it is in need so that as he grows up he will in turn feel obliged to provide for his parents when they are no longer able to care for themselves. Here too, the view of children as an investment in the future is undergoing change. Today, children are more likely to be seen as an item of consumption. We see then, although the family may be described as resting on a system of solidarity claims, these principles undergo change over time, and are highly differentiated within the family. In addition we each play different roles at different points in time. Moreover, because a long period elapses between being children, leaving the nest, and the eventual dependency of parents on children there can be no guarantee that the pattern of claims that are accepted turn out in line with what we expected them to be many years earlier. Many people who supported their own parents are surprised and disappointed when their own children do not behave in the same way.

In the economy the rationale for claims rests on the principle of contribution. In the world of those activities which we call 'work' we 'earn' what we get. Economics has developed this rationale theoretically in the form of the theory of marginal productivity; an employer will hire up to the point at which the marginal contribution of the additional worker at least equals the cost of paying him (or her) but not beyond that point; it must therefore follow that, barring insufficient information, time-lags etc., people will receive the value of what they contribute. But there is no way that this elegant reasoning can be validated empirically. In the real world, work takes the form of complex systems of collaboration within firms and between institutions; prices are set by power and by tradition as well as by supply and demand; and it is generally impossible to measure any one person's contribution to final output. In practice, people argue the equity of wages in terms of comparison. How high must miners' wages be to attract workers into mining, instead of other careers? What is an appropriate differential between wages for work as a miner at the coal-face, and work at the mine above-ground? What is the appropriate compensation for the dangers of mine work?

Because the marginalist interpretation cannot be empirically validated, and because wage determination clearly takes place in a world of social institutions, the marginalist description has been substantially criticized from many points of view. There is a large body of work on labour-market discrimination, and on segmented markets. The Marxists see wage-setting as the outcome of power struggles. Barbara Wootton long ago pointed to the high managerial salaries which she argued could only be explained in terms of the sociology of status and institutional behaviour.[9] Feminists have called attention to the body of unrenumerated and perhaps undercompensated work performed outside the labour market by women. But it is notable how closely the arguments around these issues have stuck to the underlying logic of economic productivity; for example, feminists compute the economic value of housework, and argue 'equal wages for work of equal value'.

In addition to claims around work, the claims organized within the economic realm include claims around capital. While capital may be seen as a residue of prior claims which takes the form of deferred consumption, capital and/or property become a claims structure in their own right. Return from capital enjoys a special position in the claims system, partly because it is believed that capital provides investment which makes the development of other resources uniquely possible. Thus if the well-being of a society as a whole depends on the availability of capital for investment, then government has a special responsibility to promote its availability. On the other hand, its strategic importance leads many critics to the view that more control over capital is required so that it can be brought to bear to achieve collective purposes. These claims, largely organized and institutionalized within the regulatory and policy arena which we have called the realm of the artificial, obviously represent a rather different set of claimants than the claims in the area of work, and a different sort of economic contribution. Although claims on behalf of capital are developed also according to the rationale of economic contribution and productivity, the consequences of doing so are to introduce a novel principle of social justice. As Amartya Sen puts it, 'The moral appeal of giving more to "those who are more productive and contribute more to output" does not readily translate into giving more to "those who own more productive resources which contribute more to output".' Nevertheless the social and intellectual constructions which gloss over 'these ambiguities are crucial to (the contribution principle's) moral appeal'.[10]

Government has been variously interpreted as the domain for arbitrating and reconciling claims of various groups and interests, as the instrument through which a governing class dominates and manipulates society in its interest, as a semi-autonomous cluster of institutions which interact in complex ways with the rest of society.

However we come to interpret government's social role — and it is possible that there is some truth in each of these interpretations — we must understand government as having a special role in the system of claims in two different ways. On the individual level, it constitutes the realm of claiming in the form of political and legal rights; on the collective level, government, as the institution which creates and implements policy for society, is the pre-eminent domain of the artificial. At the individual level, in the domain of rights, the rationales of claiming applied to government are derived from the appeal to citizenship. On the collective level, in the domain of public policy, the rationales of claiming are derived from the idea of the public interest.

Government as an employer is in some aspects an employer like any other, contracting and setting wages via the rationale of economic contribution. But government hiring and wage policy has a special tinge because of the potential of a special appeal, in government hiring and pay systems, to the principle of equality in citizenship.

Government as welfare provider draws legitimation from ideas both of economic management in the public interest and from social ideas in which concepts of political citizenship become translated into economic claims for support. The concept of a right to some sort of basic 'safety net' for society's members has become an established underlying principle of the claims systems of the western welfare societies, including the United States.

Again, as regulator government differentially serves the interests of different groups, but it must do so in terms of the rationale of collective purpose, and the special general-interest vocabulary of the realm of the artificial. The accommodation to conflicting claims is legitimated by appeal to a higher purpose where interests are redefined as service to the Public Interest. A system of incentives to encourage business investment is justified as contributing to general prosperity. What is good for General Motors is also for the general good.

Of course, claims couched in the vocabulary of 'rights' and

of 'public purpose', like those couched in the vocabulary of 'earnings', ebb and flow, are negotiated and renegotiated. It is in the claims against government, with the interlocking of the several rationales of political right and shared citizenship, public purpose, and economic contribution, that it is most evidently clear that we are dealing with issues of political economy.

An aspect of the process of claiming is the development of *claims rationales*. While the establishment of claims is a process of pressure, leverage, bargaining, claims are asserted in terms of normative argument. These rationales typically include both elements of factual assertion as to the nature of society (inevitability, efficiency) and elements of assertion as to the ethically proper (justice, compassion, right character). Although the claims made within the family, and against the firms and the State, interact, these are also to a substantial degree segregated from each other, in substantial part through the separation of the rationales underlying each. Thus, for example, the rationales for claims against the State are largely embedded in law and legislation and in political theory; economic theory centring on concepts of productivity plays a substantial role in developing the rationales for claims against the firms; and claiming within the family is played out against a background of loyalty and social custom and the sociological and psychological theorizing which attempts to make sense of this behaviour. The demand for 'Wages for Housework' has the power to shock, in part because it violates the traditional separations between claims rationales.

Since the various sets of claims against kin, against the State, and against firms, and their various rationales can never be completely segregated but are bound to interact with each other, the outcome of the various historic processes of claiming is what may be described as a number of distinctive *claims systems*. These claims systems may then be compared as wholes, not only with respect to the distribution of claims on quantity of economic resources (as in income-distribution studies) or security resources (as in divisions between primary and secondary workers), but also with respect to the placing of claims. One might, for example, compare societies in which the dominant claims subsystem is that of claims against firms (the domain of the economic) with those in which the dominant subsystem is that of claims against the State (government) or against kin (the family). Such a comparison would cross-cut the usual socialist-capitalist division, placing Yugoslavia, for example, in a category with some capitalist states and in contrast to more centrally managed capitalist and socialist economies. Anthropologists and sociologists have made much of the contrast between the role of kinship in pre-industrial societies and its role in the industrialized ones, in which other institutions come into being and play powerful roles.[11] This is a process in which claiming within the family, while still important, loses its dominant position in the structure of claims, and institutions organized on other principles come to dominate society. It has been pointed out that the legal systems of western industrial societies have experienced several successive waves of new kinds of 'property rights' which represent, in effect, new claimants and new possible focuses for assertion of claims. The development of business law which made possible claims in the firm was paralleled by the development of a structure of claims to the job system, such as seniority rights, which established bodies of claims for the new bourgeoisie and newly established working class, respectively; more recently, the legal system has seen the evolution of a body of claims and entitlements in the welfare system, relevant to persons at a social level below that of the established working class.

The political history of the eighteenth to the twentieth centuries in Europe has as its major theme the emergence of new claims against the State and against the firm, and the redefinition of claims against kin. To cite some conspicuous examples: the legitimizing of labour unions in the hard-fought struggle for the right to organize established a new claiming group and a claiming agenda which they promoted; the obligation of the United States federal government to provide jobs, or failing that to provide income for families of long-term unemployed workers, represented the emergence of a claim against the State inconceivable in a previous age; there has even evolved with time a much less specific, but nevertheless real claim against the State that it should so manage the economy as to produce a reasonable level of stable well-being for its citizens. In these and other ways we continue to create new claims against government (such as day care), against the economy (as in job-splitting, career lines for women, etc.), and claims within the family (as in the change of sex roles within the family). This political process also creates reactions against these claims — e.g., backlash against welfare and against the women's rights movements.

The thrust of this perspective is to see the various systems of claims as both internally negotiable and as culturally variable. A given system of claims appears in this view as a system of social conventions, or an always evolving system of power relations.

The processes by which such claims come into existence, and in some cases come to be established as legitimate, are themselves complex. Pizzorno distinguishes several distinct phases. The first is a state of 'formation of collective identities', during which 'action is not oriented toward the maximization of individual gains, but toward the aim itself of forming the new collective identities . . . During this phase, actions (like conflicts, polarization of positions, preference for ideological coherence, for "unrealistic" goals) that would appear "irrational" from the point of view of individual gains acquire a meaning if seen from the point of view of identity formation.' This is then a phase of heightened participation and militancy. But when the goal of identity recognition is achieved and the claims are legitimized, participation will subside and ideological affirmation recede.[12]

Organization by itself is not sufficient to enter effectively into the direct claiming process. What is needed is resources which compel others to recognize the claim. These resources take many forms. When the Chartists organized to make a claim for the vote, the resource they made use of was numbers. Now the power to vote in large numbers became a resource. Yet another resource, one especially available to groups with little power, is the capacity to disrupt the flow of wanted services, or the capacity to excite a sense of shame for the failure to honour a claim which appeals to widely accepted moral principles of social justice. (See Myrdal's *American Dilemma*[13] for an example applied to racial discrimination.)

But not all claiming arises from this direct process of groups organizing to make the claim on their own behalf. There is an indirect process; one group claims something on behalf of another group. For example, social workers who want to make services available to the retarded, the mentally ill, and to the otherwise disabled will lobby and proselytize for the entitlement of their potential clientele to services of this sort. The motives inspiring these claiming processes are varied, usually combining self-interest and altruism in arguments which appeal to the claims rationales existing in society. Once a claim is established — as, for example, in the entitlement of old people to social-security benefits — bodies of claims managers come into existence to manage this body of claims, and they promote their interpretation of the best interest of the claimants.[14] Some analysts see this indirect process in which claims managers intervene and reinterpret needs as a usurpation of the democratic process of interest-group negotiation.

The discussions about these indirect claiming processes — the self-interest of social workers, the role of 'outside agitators' — make it clear that there are within societies implicit standards with respect to the claiming process.

The conflicts and interdependencies between claims structures bring in response complex forms of claiming which try to take account of these conflicts and interdependencies. In the United States and Europe, organized groups have recognized that their well-being not only depends on the wages they receive, but also on the direct benefits they can secure from government, such as the indirect concessions they can win in the form of rebates and subsidies, and the burdens that can be relieved in the form of lower taxes. Unions in Britain, and to a lesser extent in the United States, in recognition of these interdependencies have bargained for a claim package which links the contractual arrangements of the firm with the legal arrangements of the State; the position of the worker may be improved by lowering his taxes, increasing his benefits, or raising his wages. As these interdependencies become the subject of bargaining, it becomes clear that we are enmeshed in larger issues about the structure of society as a whole, which we have called claims structures. When bargaining takes place at a local, or sectoral level, the issues of interdependencies are obscured because there is no national framework to give them coherence. This is the situation that prevails in the United States, where we have a highly segmented system of bargaining by interest groups. When bargaining takes place at the national level as in Britain and Sweden, then implications for the claiming process for inflation, income distribution, etc., become more evident. (Off in the wings yet another issue is the future of claims within the kinship structure and how these influence claims against the firm, as in lower wages for teenagers, and claims against the State, as in affirmative action.) A struggle between government and national interest groups thus ensues, mediated by public opinion and other interest groups — but where government is both a mediator and an actor. The character of this struggle is central to the problem of liberal democracy in an industrial state.

In the course of the negotiations around these issues of claims structure the political, the economic, and the social come to be seen as intertwined, or as aspects of a single system with respect to which policy is to be made. A theory of the economy cannot be separated from a theory of the State and a theory of the family. In moving towards this view of the field of policy, the capitalist welfare states come to a kind of convergence with the socialist countries. At the same time, within each of the categories — capitalist and socialist — there are particular national forms of claiming and claims structures, grounded in the choices and necessities of particular histories and particular situations.

Discussion of such complex and interdependent claims structures immediately raises the issue of how the system of distribution and the system of production are related to each other. It seems self-evident that distributional systems are not neutral; there is a close relationship between the structure of claims and the total production of the society. The way we slice up the pie influences the size of the pie. Moves to distribute resources according to criteria of welfare or social justice which fail to take proper account of incentives to produce run the risk of undermining the vitality of the economic system and reducing the resources available for everyone.

Neo-classical economic theory proposes a solution to the problem based on the marginalist analysis of market transactions; workers will receive wages tending to equal the value of their marginal products; the amount of wage-claims and the supply of goods and services against which claims are made is self-calibrating.

The theory is willing to accept the rough-and-tumble reality of groups negotiating and struggling for claims by acknowledging that there is a prior historic process by which wages have been set and which must be taken as given. Marginal productivity is nevertheless rescued from this disorderly process by the view that capital adjusts to the reality of the wages it faces. This reciprocal process of adjustment has the net effect of adjusting the payment of various categories of labour to their marginal productivity. In this view there need not be any conflict between marginal productivity and claiming theories.[15]

Nevertheless, if we turn from the theory to the practice, we recognize that the marginal productivity of wages, with its self-equilibrating functions, is a postulate of particular and general equilibrium and not an observation about reality.

It also obscures the fact that many workable arrangements can exist, and that those arrangements which exist are the products of particular historical struggles, and are subject to change by similar processes in the future.

Now we are talking not about individual claims in a market system, but about the claims of organized groups in the political arena. Even if individual claims in a market system are seen to be self-stabilizing, the same cannot be argued for the claims of organized groups. When groups compete to get for themselves more of the social product, they do not give back either more work or more sacrifice. They get more if they are able to threaten more. What society buys from them, in granting benefits, is 'consensus'. What is at stake in atomistic competition is the distribution of the social product in return for contribution to it. What is at stake in group competition is the distribution of the social product in return for social consensus. This gives the groups a larger portion of the social product than their members contribute (in market terms).[16]

Nevertheless, we recognize that these 'politically derived' claims structures, constituting the social and the moral framework within which economic activity takes place, must have their consequences, and important ones, for the size of the pie. But here, instead of a clear and dominant theory, we have various competing and partial theories, providing no clear guidance.

As political claims against large-scale corporatism expand, leading to more job security for some, improved quality of the work environment, the growth of fringe benefits from pensions to medical care to educational grants, we are beset with a puzzle. Shall we interpret these trends as a sign of success or a cause of failure? Do these claims erode or nourish productivity? Do they lead to less worker alienation, more collective identification, and hence to larger output (Japanese corporatism), or do they lead to undermining incentives? What kinds of corporatism lead to productivity and self-calibration — state corporatism, which we know as the welfare state, or business corporatism, we call tenure and fringes? If production and growth affect the structure of claims, then is it true, as Kristol has argued,[17] that in time the claims arising out of the growth society will erode the structure which made that growth possible?

We have now shifted, in the discussion over incentives, to a level on which micro-economic theory will not be particularly helpful. We are now dealing with claims systems as providing, as wholes, frameworks for action which will be expressed in what is produced and how it is produced. To the argument that a degree of income inequality is necessary to bring about the savings and reinvestment necessary for long-term growth is opposed R. H. Tawney's argument that the lessening of social tension and hostility produced by greater egalitarianism would be reflected in increased output.[18] To Fidel Castro's exhortation of 'creating wealth with political awareness and more collective wealth with more collective political awareness'[19] is opposed the view that it is only 'material stimulus that is indispensable to the increase in work productivity, the essential key to Cuban economic recovery'.[20]

Although there is argument over the resources available, and ongoing economic growth very much alleviates the sense of struggle over scarce resources, it is always recognized that resources are not infinite, and therefore, claims compete. For example, when affirmative action opens jobs for Blacks and women, Whites and men feel threatened. The claim of women for pay equal to that of men's for similar work conflicts with the press for equality of income as between families — since better-paid women are quite likely to be married to better-paid men.

This problem, in turn, surfaces as an issue of latent conflict between two sorts of rationale which have been applied to earnings: the economic rationale of payment for a factor of production, and the welfare rationale expressed in the phrase 'a living wage', related to the concept that earnings should be sufficient to support a family.[21]

Not only do claims conflict, but the legitimating rationales of claims systems are potentially competitive. In the capitalist United States, conservatives express concern that rise in welfare benefits will erode work incentive. The debates within socialism over 'moral' versus 'material' incentives centre around the understanding that the use of the classic 'bourgeois mechanisms' of career openings and consumer goods to shape the quantity, quality, and allocation and discipline of the labour force leads necesarily to the privatization of social life and away from general commitment to the polity and to the life of politics. Systems such as the Cuban and the Chinese, which have invested heavily in the construction of politicized claims structures, have necessarily restricted the role of the classic 'economic' claims even while focusing closely on the role of work.

The discussion is made even more complex because the level of affluence and the rate at which it grows influence how the pie is distributed. In periods of economic growth there is more to distribute. Because it is not necessary to take from some to give to others it is not necessary to worry about relativities. 'The growth alternative is inherently less divisive . . . it offers the possibility of consensus action, of a game with winners but no absolute losers, of levelling up without levelling down; limiting the political choice to distributing the increment, rather than demanding the more fundamental political act of redistributing existing resources.'[22]

This raises a set of questions. Is it true, as the proponents of political 'overload' argue, that there is a danger of claims exceeding the resources available to satisfy them? The argument is that the political process has no automatic way, like markets, of equilibrating claims to resources; in the bid for votes, politicians will promise more than the system can deliver, passing the overdraft on to future generations via dissaving, or to the current one via inflation. In the same vein, those who see a tight ceiling to resources, see every claim as displacing another claim. In both views there is a general issue as to the limits of claiming.

We are sure that there must be in the long run, limits to claiming, in that we cannot spend more than we have. But we are equally sure that the limits are highly indeterminate, for several reasons. First, as we have noted, the very nature of the claiming system shapes incentives, and thus, over time, the size of the pie; but these relationships, both between claims systems and incentives, and between incentives and the size of the pie, are certainly not understood and probably also indeterminate. Second, not all the resources of a society need to be subject to institutionalized claims. Societies permit greater and lesser degrees of stabilized claims; one of the characteristics of mature industrial societies is the growth of the structure of shelters provided by the State and the firm. Therefore, in a given society, claims may take the form of stabilizing what was formerly insecurity, rather than taking away an institutionalized shelter from someone else. Thus we believe that there must be limits; but no one really knows where these limits are. Therefore the process of claiming takes place in the context of uncertainty as to the limits of possibility. Any definition of limits is itself part of the claiming process.

But who is debating these issues, and in what settings are they debating them? The debates about such issues take place in what we have called the realm of the artificial: the intellectul construction which sets off those aspects of society which are the subject of policy, of societal management. The realm of the artificial includes institutionally the policy-making and planning bodies of government, as well as the academic institutions of policy analysis which see government policy as their sphere of influence. Policy analysis may be interpreted as a set of activities in which claims and claim rationales are organized within this domain of the artificial.

The ground rules of policy analysis require an appeal to

scientific laws, to empirical evidence, and to reason and logic. But, as we have argued, the social sciences do not provide a determinate basis from which a value and interest neutral policy analysis might spring. The very analysis of the claiming process, and of the issues which arise in debate, requires a language of understanding which itself reflects interests and shapes claims.

Therefore, within the realm of the artificial, as within the realm of the natural, there are concealed interests and ongoing claims. But to fully surface these concealed interests is to undermine the legitimacy of the debate itself. 'Civil servants and managers alike justify themselves and their claims to authority, power and money by invoking their own competence as scientific managers of social change.'[23]

Claims from above and claims from below seem to be represented in different ways within this realm of the artificial, the domain of expertise. Claims from above may appear in the form of the analysis of system-requiredness. It is the very assumption of requiredness which contains all the baggage of claim establishment, within which the earlier discussion of claim overload must be understood.

NOTES

[1] Karl Polanyi, *The Great Transformation*, Boston: Beacon Press, 1957.
[2] For a review of such concepts in relation to developing countries, see Gunnar Myrdal, *Asian Drama*, New York: Pantheon Books, 1968, pp. 1843-7. For a version within developed society context, see Thomas Vietorisz and Bennett Harrison, 'Labor Market Segmentation: Positive Feedback and Divergent Development', *American Economic Review*, vol. lxiii, No. 2, May 1973, pp. 366-76.
[3] Suzanne Berger and Michael Piore, *Dualism and Discontinuity in Industrial Societies*, Cambridge; Cambridge University Press, 1980.
[4] Frank Knight, 'Anthropology and Economics', *Journal of Political Economy*, Vol. 49, 1940, pp. 247-68.
[5] Laboratoire d'économie et le sociologie du travail, 'Comparaison de hiérarchie des salaires entre l'Allemagne et la France' (unpublished), Aix-en-Provence, 31 December 1972.
[6] Joel Feinberg, 'The Nature and Value of Rights', *Journal of Value Inquiry*, vol. iv, No. 4, Winter 1970, pp. 243-57; Marcia Freedman, *Labor Markets: Segments and Shelters*, Montclair, New Jersey: Allanheld, Osmun, 1976; Amartya Sen, *Poverty and Famines: An Essay on*

Entitlement and Deprivation, Oxford: Clarendon Press, 1981.

[7] Martin Rein and Lee Rainwater, 'Sources of Family Income and the Determinants of Welfare', Joint Center for Urban Studies of MIT and Harvard University, May 1976.

[8] Charles Reich, 'The New Property', *The Yale Law Journal*, Vol. 73, No. 5, April 1964, pp. 733–86.

[9] Barbara Wootton, *The Social Foundations of Wage Policy*, London: Unwin University Books, 1962.

[10] Amartya Sen, 'Just Deserts', *New York Review of Books*, No. 3, 4 March 1982, p. 4.

[11] Robert Redfield, 'The Folk Society', *American Journal of Sociology*, vol. lii, No. 4, Jan. 1947.

[12] Alessandro Pizzorno, 'Civil Society, State and Pluralism', Princeton, New Jersey, 1978 (unpublished).

[13] Gunnar Myrdal, *An American Dilemma: The Negro Problem and Modern Democracy*, N.Y. London, Harper & Bros. 1944.

[14] Martha Derthick, *Policy Making for Social Security*, Washington DC: The Brookings Institute, 1979.

[15] In our understanding of marginal productivity theory we were substantially assisted by discussions with John Harris and Robert Solow.

[16] John Rawls, *A Theory of Justice*, Cambridge, Mass.: Belknap Press of Harvard University Press, 1971.

[17] Irving Kristol, *Two Cheers for Democracy*, New York: Basic Books, 1977.

[18] R. H. Tawney, *Equality*, London: Allen and Unwin, 1952.

[19] Fidel Castro, 'Creating Wealth with Political Awareness, not Creating Political Awareness with Money or Wealth', Havana, *Granma*, 28 July 1968.

[20] Rene Dumont, *Cuba: Socialism and Development*, New York: Grove Press, 1970, p. 140.

[21] Fred Hirsch, *The Social Limits of Growth*, Cambridge: Harvard University Press, 1976, p. 174.

[22] Gertrude Williams, 'The Myth of "Fair" Wages', *Economic Journal*, vol. lxvi, 1956, p. 174.

[23] Alastair McIntyre, *After Virtue: A Study in Moral Theory*, Notre Dame Indiana: University of Notre Dame Press, 1981, p. 82.

CHAPTER 3

Housework: Women in the Domestic Economy

WE have argued that societies develop institutionalized systems of claims: that claims made in the world of work ('earnings', 'wages') should be looked at in the same framework as claims against the State or within the family system; and that back of every system of explicit claims is a set of conceptualizations as to the 'natural' which govern entitlements via implicit understandings as to normal roles, appropriate personal characteristics, and just deserts. If we now turn to women's claims within the family structure, and the relationship of this part of the claiming system to women's claims in other realms, these points at once become manifest.

When we look at women's participation in paid employment, we have no difficulty in understanding why it is that women's labour-force attachment is weaker than men's, why it is that so many of them work intermittently or part time, why their drive to shape a long-term career is weaker, why it is that they are particularly interested in flexitime arrangements. It is women's 'domestic responsibilities' which have to be dealt with, alongside paid employment. It is impossible to understand women's claims in either the public or the private sphere without reference to the conventional understanding that there is housework to be done, and that women are pre-eminently responsible for doing it, either as hired servants or, in a society in which hired servants are rare, as housewives.

Here, too, we encounter at once the realm of the natural. We find ourselves pitched into a universe of discourse altogether different from that of wage-bargaining and fair return: a discourse of social roles, interpersonal responsibility, and commitment. Work is performed, and support is extended, but we speak of family ties, home-making, masculinity and femininity, love and marriage.

But these activities which we tend to think of as an aspect of social role, and therefore outside the realm of economic calculation, if treated in economic terms would appear as no small matter.

Calculating the economic value of housework is essentially problematic. Should we value it in terms of the cost of providing the services on the market, or in terms of opportunity cost, i.e. what the housewife could have made if she had been working for pay? Each of these modes of calculation presents alternatives; market costs can be estimated as the replacement cost of the housework carried out by a generalist or via a service-cost approach which imagines specialists — a cook, a laundress, a chauffeur — taking over the functions. Opportunity costs may be calculated firstly in terms of gross compensation, secondly in terms of net wages, or thirdly in terms of net return (where working costs are deducted).

The Bureau of Economic Analysis recently attempted to estimate the value of these different measures. In 1976 the value of housework through a market-cost approach came to $566 billion to hire the individual to do general housework (replacement cost) as compared to $789 billion to hire market specialists (service-cost approach). The replacement cost equals about 33 per cent of GNP and the service cost about 46 per cent.

When we focus on opportunity costs, the value is much larger. Thus over a trillion dollars ($1,037 billion) is spent if the measure is based on gross compensation; $887 billion is spent if on net compensation; and $777 billion is spent on net return. Expressed as a percentage of GNP, gross compensation equals 61 per cent of GNP, net compensation 52 per cent, and net return 46 per cent.

In brief, we can say that if we try to hire someone to do our housework, the cost is about a third of GNP; if we figure the housewife's labour in terms of net return after deducting taxes and the cost of working, it's about 46 per cent of GNP. These are astronomical figures.[1]

A housewife is a woman: a housewife does housework . . . The characteristic features of the housewife role in modern industrialized society are 1) its *exclusive allocation to women*, rather than to adults of both sexes; 2) its association with *economic dependence*, i.e. with the dependent role of the woman in modern marriage; 3) *its status as non-work* — or its opposition to 'real', i.e. economically productive work, and 4) its *primacy* to women, that is, its priority over other roles.²

Only very recently has a study of how men and women spend their time seemed to show any substantial decrease in women's family work, and a tendency for the total work week of employed wives and husbands to show a rough equality in hours.³ In general, the double day has been the consequence of the continuing commitment to housekeeping by women who also contribute to family income through paid employment. Similarly, other participation in public life by women encounters the competition of 'household duties'. In Cuba in 1968 there was, as part of the general societal mobilization, an interest in engaging women in political life. But, the leaders of the Federation of Women said, very few women were party members. The problem was that women who had to add on to a working day a shopping activity complicated by standing in lines, and the preparation of dinner and its subsequent clean-up, for which men were still reluctant to share the burden, found the idea of attending meetings in the evening an impossible overload. Eventually the Cuban leadership tackled the problem of these conflicting claims by introducing measures to equalize responsibility for the domestic sphere.

In the United States, the conditions for doing housework are no doubt easier than they were in Cuba in 1968. But here we have to note that housework is peculiar in the relationship between labour time and technology. Within the last century, the technology of housework has been completely transformed. 'In a six-day experiment conducted in 1899 by Boston's School of Housekeeping, 5 hours and 26 minutes were spent on caring for a coal stove: sifting coal, laying and tending the fire, emptying ashes, carrying coal, and blacking the stove to guard against rust. This was compared to 10 minutes of fire-tending and 1½ hours of cleaning for a gas stove . . . . Wood required more tending than coal: furthermore, the stove used in the experiment was an advanced model.'⁴ Less than a hundred years ago, clothing and linens were boiled and wrung and hung and ironed by hand; clothing was made at home; commercial food preservation was in its infancy, so that canning in a hot kitchen dominated women's summers; although mechanical refrigerators were established as desirable by the mid-nineteenth century, it was a long time before they became commonplace in US homes.[5]

Yet, although housewives had no doubt a long and arduous working day, they managed to fit it all in while rearing children, going to socials, and eating and sleeping. With refrigerators a commonplace, mechanical washer-dryers, canned and frozen foods, central heating, gas and electric ranges, and a variety of mechanical gadgets, one would imagine that housework would (a) take up only a tiny fraction of any woman's day and (b) at least take much less time than in societies where this technology is not available on the same scale.

The evidence shows the opposite.

In the 1960's, suitable large-scale empirical data on how much time women actually spend doing housework began to become available. Results of these studies challenged the characterization of technology shrinking the demands of housework. Morgan *et al.* found families with more automatic home appliances estimating more hours of housework than those with fewer appliances . . . Robinson *et al.* found employed women in the United States with much higher ownership of appliances spending only about four fewer hours per week on housework than employed women in Yugoslavia or Poland and more time doing housework than employed women in Bulgaria and Peru . . . .

The results dovetailed with historical comparisons made with results of earlier, usually cruder, time-use studies. Women both in and out of the labor market reported virtually the same amount of time doing housework in the 1960's as they had ten, twenty, or forty years previously . . . Vanek (1974) found the number of weekly hours on housework by housewives to vary only from 51 hours in 1926 to 52 hours in 1929, 1936 and 1943 to 53 hours in 1953 and 55 hours in 1965-66.[6]

Thus while still more recent time studies show hours spent on housework diminishing, there appears to be 'no systematic tendency for women with household technology to spend less time doing housework'.[7] A drop in routine cleaning, and a slight drop in time spent with children, even on a per-child basis, accompanied by a rise in time spent cooking, suggests that there is more at work here than a simple struggle to get through a set of daily tasks given by the necessities of household maintenance.

As Ann Oakley concluded, after interviewing housewives about their working days: 'Silly it may be, but it is only by considering the way women define their job as housewives that the housewife's long working hours can be understood.'[8]

'Keeping house is in many ways the most singular of all occupations', says Theodore Caplow in his comments on housework[9] in *The Sociology of Work*. 'By its informality, its irrationality, and its cultural importance, the whole situation of the housewife stands in violent contrast to the rest of the occupational system ... The system of motivation attached to the work of the housewife bears no resemblance to any other.'[10] Caplow goes on to point out that housework is the only current occupation in which selection bears no relationship either to natural ability or to social status, and that remuneration (if one may use the term) is inversely related to effort, for wives of wealthy men, provided with ample dress allowances and other spending money, are also likely to have both servants and an assortment of labour-saving appliances.

In terms of normal economic analysis, these are fairly staggering comments. In recent years traditional economics has sometimes conceded that consideration of commitment and obligation may disturb the tidiness of analysis based on the assumption of optimizing behaviour, but it has been content to live with such criticisms because the criticisms have been regarded as tiny exceptions to the general situation. Yet here we have a situation — and one which we earlier showed accounts for between one-third and one-half of GNP — where the normal conclusions apparently do not apply at all. There is no rational division of labour, no tendency for work done to relate to skills, and no relation of effort to renumeration — unless an additional structure of theory, as in the 'new household economics', gives an explanation to what appears as personal motive and interpersonal relationship.

Indeed, the term remuneration is itself applied with extreme awkwardness to this peculiar occupation. Housework as a set of actions is embedded in the structure of women's claims within the family as part of the reciprocal obligations between husband and wife in which men are traditionally required to provide support. Both these obligations are established in US legal tradition. Neither the legal emancipation of women, nor the entry of women into the labour force, has weakened substantially the legal status of the husband's duty to support.[11] There also appears to be in good standing an obligation on the part of married women to do housework, as in the Connecticut court's ruling in 1962 (*Rucci* v. *Rucci*) that a wife must both be a solicitous helpmeet and perform 'her household and domestic duties ... without compensation therefore. A husband is entitled to the benefit of his wife's industry and economy.'[12]

Nevertheless, while the obligations are structurally reciprocal, and a feminist book of 1909 analysed 'Marriage as a Trade',[13] the courts have steadfastly refused to view them in the model of economic exchange and remuneration for services.[14] In *Marvin* v. *Marvin* the California court held that a partner in a non-marital cohabitation arrangement might receive the reasonable value of household services rendered less the value of support received *if* it could be shown that the services were rendered with the expectation of monetary reward. Indeed, in this landmark decision the court 'rejected the invitation to modify existing community property law [applying to marriage] relying instead upon doctrines drawn from the laws of contract, trust, partnership and restitution'.[15]

The legal ideas surrounding marriage make it extraordinarily difficult, if not impossible, to take this contractual approach when people live together in legal marriage. As a consequence, in divorce cases women's claims to support have been based on such issues as marital fault, need of the wife, ability to pay of the husband, and length of the marriage (understood as bringing concomitant problems of readjustment), rather than on the value of the services performed within marriage. It is virtually impossible for a wife, within marriage, to enforce a higher level of support from her husband on the basis of the value of her housework or on any other basis.

Because a wife is obligated to provide domestic services for her husband, the courts have refused to enforce contracts under which she was to receive compensation for her labor. The courts have reasoned that if a wife already owes these services to her husband, a contract in which she is to be paid for them is void for lack of consideration. The courts have thus refused to honor contracts in which the husband agreed to pay the wife for housekeeping, entertaining, child care or other 'wifely tasks'.[16]

The courts have refused to enforce agreements between spouses in which the wife gave up a right to support.[17]

On the other hand, it would appear that the fact that the wife, through paid employment, is contributing to family support does not in itself free her from some customary or conventional obligation to do housework. Women who are employed outside the home continue to be largely responsible for child care, cooking, dishwashing, and so forth,[18] although when a woman is employed her husband is more likely to share the housework. However, one study found that a husband's family time is independent of the wife's employment status when the age and number of children are controlled.[19] It thus appears that while female employment does affect the amount of tasks that a woman has the time to accomplish, it does not actually alter the allocation of the chores between husband and wife.[20]

Thus while the domestic obligations of the housewife may be said to be structurally reciprocal to the husband's obligation to support, the two obligations are in no respect calibrated against each other in a way which would make the term 'remuneration' appropriate. 'Wages for housework' would be a definite innovation. Thus we see that while it is possible to describe the division of labour in the family as reciprocal claims — for domestic services, for support — both law and custom embed these implicit claims within 'natural' family organization and the 'nature' of women.

In a sense, Caplow brings the conceptual problems of analysing housework on himself by dealing with the activity — at length, and interestingly — in a book on the sociology of work. A more conventional strategy in sociology is to deal with the peculiarities of housework by treating the actual activity as an aspect of social role, rather than as a part of the occupational system. (This is the approach of Lopata's *Occupation: Housewife*, for example.) As Ann Oakley puts it, in studies of the 1950s and 1960s, 'the dominant conception was one of housework as an aspect of the marital relationship'.[21] Certainly the publications which serve as trade or professional journals for this atypical occupation (*Woman's Day*, *Good Housekeeping*, and the like) combine, like those of no other, articles on technique and technology ('Space-Saving Kitchens', 'Mouth-Watering Chocolate Desserts') with articles on the self-presentation of the practitioner ('25 Prettiest Hairstyles') and on interpersonal relations ('Mothers and Daughters Who Can't Get Along', 'Can This Marriage Be Saved?').

An Italian study of domestic labour points out that the motives around housework are so thoroughly mixed that it is hard to tell burden from reward. Italian women typically use the word 'sacrifice' in speaking of child care. But 'there is also embedded in it a dimension of pleasure, of gratification, of reward which can be seen as a payment'. 'Pleasure and sacrifice go hand in hand and cannot be divided or distinguished in a clear cut way.'[22]

One way to interpret these peculiarities of housework: its relative imperviousness to criteria of technical efficiency, its personalism, its embeddedness in social role, is as cultural survival.[23] After all, we must recognize that at one time all human productive and life-maintaining activities had these same characteristics. In the small primitive community, the division of labour was largely by age and sex: as Caplow points out for housework 'the same job requirements imposed on morons and on . . . [those] of superior intelligence'. There was no sharp distinction between work and leisure. Activities were carried out in terms of interpersonal relations and social roles, rather than in terms of definite economic rewards. Such characteristics of the organization of labour applied equally to hunting, planting, tool-making, and cooking. Only with respect to the latter does this way of doing things still persist.

An alternative way of interpreting the peculiarities of housework among the occupations of the present is to see the occupation in its present state as a new creation, the artifact of economic development, the flip side of the transformation which has given most productive and life-maintaining activities an organization sharply different from that of housework. This is the interpretation of Eli Zaretsky and other neo-Marxists. 'The organization of production in capitalist society is predicated upon the existence of a certain form of family life. The wage labour system (socialized production under capitalism) is sustained by the socially necessary but private labour of housewives and mothers.'[24] Historically, he argues, the modern family is as much a recent historical creation as is the factory and wage-labour. 'Before capitalism, material production was understood, like sexuality and reproduction, to be "natural" — precisely what human beings shared with animals.'[25]

As in pre-capitalist society, throughout most of capitalist history the family has been the basic unit of 'economic' production — not the wage-earning father, but the household as a whole. While there was an intense division of labour *within* the family, based upon age, sex and family position, there was scarcely a division *between* the family and the world of commodity production, at least not until the nineteenth century. Certainly women were excluded from the few 'public' activities that existed — for example, military affairs. But their sense of themselves as 'outside' the larger society was fundamentally limited by the fact that 'society' was overwhelmingly composed of family units based upon widely dispersed, individually owned productive property . . . .

With the rise of industry, capitalism 'split' material production between its socialized forms (the sphere of commodity production) and the private labour performed predominantly by women within the home. In this form male supremacy, which long antedated capitalism, became an institutional part of the capitalist system of production.

This 'split' between the socialized labour of the capitalist enterprise and the private labour of women in the home is closely related to a second 'split' — between our 'personal' lives and our place within the social division of labour.[26]

While housewives and mothers continued their traditional tasks of production — housework, child-rearing, etc. — their labour was devalued through its isolation from the socialized production of surplus value. In addition, housewives and mothers were given new responsibility for maintaining the emotional and psychological realm of personal relations.[27]

Those whose intellectual references lie on the other side of the political spectrum will at once recognize this account as the political economy version of Talcott Parsons's interpretation of the family, in which an occupational world of rational appraisal and striving for status mobility is only made possible by protecting the family from the stress which goes with competition between members. Thus, it follows, wives must not go in for occupational striving themselves, but have the responsibility for preserving the family as a 'haven in a heartless world'.[28]

Zaretsky emphasizes the production of goods and services within the family: Talcott Parsons emphasizes the structuring of interpersonal sentiments. Both of them are talking about aspects of housework. 'The system of motivation attached to the work of the housewife' which, Caplow says, 'bears no resemblance to any other' occupation is peculiar in its particular joining of sentiment and service.

Caplow interprets the combination in a Parsonian framework.

Strictly speaking the economic functions of the housewife are interchangeable with those of the domestic servant, and literal substitution is usually possible. To avoid this menial identification (which is insupportable under the general requirement that the class status of all members of the conjugal family be the same), it is necessary to attach great importance to the difference in emotional quality between the work of the housewife and that of the servant. This device is not entirely successful ... On the other hand, the emotional aura surrounding housework is so intensified by this manner of regarding it that any rationalization of functions (the establishment of cooperative kitchens in housing projects, for example) is seriously hampered.[29]

It should be possible to go somewhat beyond this simple functionalist avoidance-of-conflict interpretation of housework. To understand the meaning of housework for women's — and men's — lives, it seems necessary to look more closely at the various elements which go into housework, and the way in which they appear to have been changing. One way to begin this would be to look at the allocation of time to specific activities for a sample of housewives at different points in history. We cannot do this, for we do not have such a body of data. The material which does exist[30] goes back less than two decades. Thus it seems necessary to take a more qualitative approach, and to draw some generalizations about the content and character of housework from what has been written on the history of the family and of gender roles.

In this consideration it seems useful to distinguish conceptually between three components of housework: the production of goods and services of daily domestic use, child-rearing, and status-defining activities. These components will, of course, be intermixed in practice; for example, the preparation of meals, the education of children, interior furnishing

Housework: Women in the Domestic Economy 47

and its upkeep, will all be affected (and require heavier inputs of housekeeping time) in a family which is oriented around issues of social status. But to explain why it is that housework continues to require so many hours of time, despite the extraordinary transformation of its technology, it seems necessary to call attention to issues other than the simple daily necessities which call on the housewife's time and attention as cooking and washing get easier.

The production and rearing of children has always been a part of housework, combined in various ways with the other activities of a woman's day. (Indeed, one of the troubles with the old-fashioned coal or wood cooking-stove, it appears, was not simply the time spent stoking and cleaning already referred to, but also the vigilance required to keep small children from burning themselves.) At one time, writers on the family liked to see child care as a diminishing responsibility for women, a dwindling component of housework. In this supposed diminution of the labours of child care, technological advance — the diaper service, the modern stove — took a poor second to the school system. It was the advent of universal public education which, it was believed, had taken much of the responsibility for socialization of children 'out of the family', thus, by implication, relieving the burdens of the housewife.

More recently, a different interpretation of the educational story makes the school the cutting edge of a new view of childhood which has as its inevitable consequence a new burden on the housewife.

The great event was . . . the revival, at the beginning of modern times, of an interest in education . . .

Henceforth it was recognized that the child was not ready for life, and that he had to be subjected to a special treatment, a sort of quarantine, before he was allowed to join the adults.

This new concern about education would gradually install itself in the heart of society and transform it from top to bottom. The family ceased to be simply an institution for the transmission of a name and an estate — it assumed a moral and spiritual function, it moulded bodies and souls. The care expended on children inspired new feelings, a new emotional attitude . . .[31]

The modern family . . . cuts itself off from the world and opposes to society the isolated group of parents and children. All the energy of the group is expended on helping the children rise in the world ...

This evolution from the medieval family to the seventeenth-century family and then to the modern family was limited for a long time to the nobles, the middle class, the richer artisans and the richer labourers ... Family life finally embraced nearly the whole of society, to such an extent that people have forgotten its aristocratic and middle-class origins.[32]

In the late nineteenth century we find established in the United States a 'new conception of children as precious, and different from adults' and the accompanying idea that it was the mother who was not only the bearer but chief rearer of the children, responsible for carrying out this high 'civilizing' mission.[33] 'Some women were so self-conscious about their responsibilities as mothers that their concern bordered on anxiety.'[34] The subsequent advent of the concept of 'expertise' in child-rearing and the production of manuals of professional advice may be said to have moved child care into the realm of the artificial. However, child care was still set in the 'natural' responsibility of women for mothering; the advent of expertise seems, rather than easing the performance of the child-rearing task, to have further elevated its status and the level of performance assumed to be appropriate.[35]

This set of changes in consciousness and in domestic practice may be put in a political-economy framework by connecting them with changes in the requirements for labour towards a higher level of skill; it is no longer possible, for the family in its role of social reproduction, to put an unfinished product on the market. While this is partly reflected in the extension of formal schooling (and thus the loss of children's contribution in doing housework — see Minge-Klevana), it is presumably also reflected in parents', especially mother's, inputs to children's education and general socialization.

Another aspect of housework which seems to have received less sociological notice is the production of those physical settings and social events which help to define the family's social status.[36] The blending and confusion of the elements of expensiveness and of beauty which Veblen identified as 'pecuniary standards of taste'[37] is no less characteristic of the tasteful middle-class home for its being rendered in an informal beam and butcher-block style evoking the country home — itself a natural theme for conspicuous display. More critical for housework is the programmatic aspect of conspicuous emulation. The idea of 'entertaining' as a status-maintaining display of both wealth and taste is, of course, not new: but it was once the prerogative of princes, and carried out by large staffs of servants. 'Entertaining' has been democratized; it is now among the status-maintaining functions of the household well down in the class structure, even if restrained by the idea of the impropriety of excess;[38] and with the disappearance of domestic servants, the task of both programming and execution falls on the housewife.

The three aspects of housework which we have distinguished conceptually — production of goods and services for use by members of the household, child-rearing, and status display — are phenomenologically intertwined. One could examine the evolution of status display behaviour, and its tendency to dominate the production of goods and services for domestic consumption, by looking at the way the American kitchen has evolved from a utilitarian workshop to a centre of ingenious interior decoration left at least partially open to the living-room for the attention of guests.

But it would certainly increase our difficulty in understanding the hold of housework over women if we thought of all this as simply forced upon women by their husbands, by men in general, or by society as a whole. We may think of it as a form of job inflation. The elaboration of the necessary in the sphere of housework also has its positive attractions, to which the sense of audience, implicit in the concepts of the 'house beautiful' and of 'creative cookery', must contribute substantially. The dramatic production is to the audience an experience to be enjoyed; to the actors, set designers, director, and producer it is an act of creation. Housework also develops commitment in its practitioners as a realm of creativity and artistic expression. While the philosopher Baker Brownell[39] is perhaps unique in treating style in cookery within the framework of a theory of aesthetics, there would appear to be no a priori reason for not doing so, and a dinner-party is a piece of performing art like a ballet. Housekeeping thus provides a potential area of creativity, and one fully open to amateur efforts.

The various constituent components of housework are given a unity by their common setting within domestic architecture and by the economic logic in which 'anyone assigned to a high-frequency non-postponable task in the household becomes like a fixed factor of production'[40] so that it appears natural for 'the woman of the house' to take charge of a heterogeneous set of tasks having as their only similarity their requirement of being dealt with more or less immediately.[41] It comes to appear that the binding-up of children's scratched knees, tutoring on the multiplication table, and the polishing of silver are natural elements in the 'housewife's job'. Furthermore, the pooling of these disparate elements in the housewife's role is facilitated by their common attribution of meaning in terms of interpersonal relations within the family. It is possible for an economist to look at housework as the non-monetized production of goods and services, but commitment to housework by women is established on the basis of the symbolism of housework as the affirmation of commitment to other family members. Associated with the property of being perpetually 'on call' as a 'fixed factor of production' is the property of being 'on call' in the sense of responsibility for and commitment to the members of the household. 'Nothin' says lovin' like something from the oven' was the Pillsbury Flour sales slogan. The goods and services produced within the household are not simple equivalents to those which might be purchased.

> Consider an example of a chocolate cake baked by a member of a household. Within the neoclassical approach, that cake has value proportional to the sum of the market goods and time inputs evaluated at their market prices. Now, take the same cake and assume that it was baked for the birthday of one of the household members. The inputs of market goods and time are precisely the same, but there is good reason to value the cake differently. That is, the chocolate cake produced as a relatively routine dessert may be roughly equivalent in value to an apple pie. But when *defined* as a birthday cake, its value may be significantly enhanced.
>
> ... Birthdays come once a year by social convention and would lose their meaning if they occurred more frequently. This implies that the value of birthday cakes depends in part on an 'artificial' constraint on supply that in turn increases their value ...
>
> Second, the birthday cake has *meaning* perhaps affecting its value. The cake communicates to the recipient that someone cares and may also serve to reinforce affective relationships, family loyalty, and a feeling of safety. In other words, the cake has symbolic content ....[42]

One of the consequences of the women's movement is the direction of attention to housework as work, and as having social importance.

Marxist economics treats housework in a framework of social reproduction and unpaid labour. The New Home Economics, the neo-classical version,[43] treats the household as a 'small factory'. In the traditional view, production takes place in firms, consumption in households. In the New Home Economics household commodities, not market goods, are the immediate sources of utility.

There is in this literature also a set of papers dealing with marriage as a bargain, and the division of labour in families as explicable not in terms of culture, but in terms of wage and productivity differentials. Both literatures produce difficulties for the women's movement. The Marxist literature explains housework in terms of social functionalism; it has no way of describing or accounting for the motives of housewives except as a kind of epiphenomenal false consciousness. And the policy alternative offered for women is the alienated work of the market-place.
for women is the alienated work of the market-place.

The New Home Economics also has trouble with the problem of motives, which appears as a difficulty in explaining the value of the personalized non-commodities which are the product of housework (the chocolate-cake problem). The analysis of the marriage bargain and division of labour,[44] which explains away exploitation, raises much the same problems for women as Parsonian theory. (Since women's time is worth less in the market than men's, it makes sense for them to stick to housework.)

Since the goods and services produced via housework are not simply non-monetized equivalents of commercial commodities but are also the symbolic expression of interpersonal commitments, the commitment of women to housework becomes part of women's specialization in interpersonal relations, and the evolution of women's 'domestic responsibilities' a subtopic of the evolution of the modern family and of the interpersonal sentiments which it defines as normal. This is not the place to trace the processes by which 'affection and inclination, love and sympathy came to take the place of "instrumental" considerations in regulating the dealings of family members with one another'[45] and in which during the last century in the American family the focus shifted from the tie between mother and children to that between husband and wife.[46] But each step of this process has been such as to shift the meaning of housework, and to shift it in such a way as to make possible the interpretation of its simplification, devolution to others, or elimination as the denial of love and nurturance.

When we further understand that women are socialized so as to be emotionally expressive and nurturing,[47] and to establish their social identity and to derive their own self-worth from being nurturing, it will be clear why it is difficult to shift the burden of housework from women's shoulders. The laundromat may do the clothes, and wash-and-dry eliminate the starching and ironing, but many women will use the freed time to create more sophisticated dinners.

> The woman who is employed outside her home often asks herself whether she is not putting an undue strain on her husband by expecting him to give a hand with domestic chores while other men are free after office hours either to rest, or to enjoy recreation, or to do some work which may help them to advance in their own careers. Is she, perhaps, too absorbed in her own affairs to be the wholehearted and devoted listener he expects? Is she a good enough housewife? The traditional standards of domestic virtues have not changed very much since the days of our grandmothers. The ideal housewife is still thought of as a woman who spends a maximum amount of time and labour at home, doing whatever is possible with her own hands. Though glossy journals may be full of alluring advertisements illustrating luscious dishes prepared in a jiffy out of a tin, there is, nevertheless, still a certain stigma attached to the use of the tin-opener as a kitchen utensil. Obviously a woman who spends her day at an office cannot devote the same amount of care to the preparation of meals as a full-time housewife and her cakes, bought at a shop or made from a 'Ready-Mix', will not compare with those her husband remembers with nostalgia from his mother's home.[48]

The syllogism that 'A housewife is a woman: a housewife does housework'[49] is thus not simply a set of conventional rules and social forms. It is built into women. Claims are embedded in roles: and through complex patterns of socialization roles are built in to character. Doing housework comes to be experienced as natural. Under the circumstances in which housework is performed, it will be in the nature of women to be better at housework than men. They will be better at housework because they are more nurturing persons, and housework has become a vehicle for interpersonal nurturing. It will then appear that the particular skills and interests required for successful performance of housework come more naturally to women than to men.

The interaction between women's claims in the family and in the world of work thus takes place on more than one level. There are the competing demands of the meeting and the dirty dishes; there are also interactions between ideas of women's nature developed in the family's division of labour by sex, and the division of labour in the paid economy.

The attributes which women are believed to possess which make them, it is thought, especially adaptable to housework are also thought to govern their adaptability to work outside the home. Women's 'docility' makes them particularly suitable for tedious work; their patience with small detail makes them adept at electrical assembly; women's nurturing qualities make them suited to nursery-school teaching, while they are unfit for administrative and managerial positions.

The social appraisal of women's jobs which makes it possible for the Department of Labor to classify the work of a foster mother as equal in skill requirements to those of a rest-room attendant, and that of a nursery-school teacher as requiring less skill than that of a marine-animal handler or hotel clerk, arises 'partly, no doubt, because in the past women's "unpaid" work was taken for granted, looked simple, and was not thought to need any particular formal education or training'.[50]

What are the possible strategies for dealing with housework?

One solution is to take housework, or much of it, out of the home: laundries, restaurants, day-care centres. In the nineteenth century, some American feminists attempted to socialize housework in a variety of women-run, collective enterprises: Dolores Hayden[51] tells us how this movement came into being, and how it sank out of existence beneath the encroaching flood of one-family suburban housing. Its modern counterpart is commercial: fast foods, laundromats, nursery schools. No doubt each of these modern institutions has eased the burden for at least some women, but it has hardly taken from women the special weight of 'domestic responsibilities'.

Another is the renegotiation of the division of labour within the family: husbands do more housework. Here feminists are beginning to point out there is still a responsibility problem; women do more, and in any case, they appear as responsible, delegating 'their' tasks. Men may dry dishes, but who plans dinner? When a child is sick, who stays home from work? Who has the 'labour-force attachment' and who the attachment to the family?

The demand for 'Wages for Housework' has been put forward in very diverse contexts, and with very diverse intent. On the one hand, it figures as a proposal for an income-support programme in the same family of policies as Aid to Dependent Children and family allowances.[52] In this version, it attracts the criticism of feminists[53] who see the proposed homemakers' stipends, even if technically available to men, as yet another way of entrenching the conventional sexual division of labour and the linkages woman–housewife–housework.

In another version, the demand is in itself a way of attacking conventional ideas of womanhood and women's role and 'domestic duties'.

It is the demand by which our nature ends and our struggle begins because just to want wages for housework means to refuse that work as the expression of our nature ...

To say that we want wages for housework is to espouse the fact that housework is already money for capital, that capital has made and makes money out of our cooking, smiling, fucking. At the same time, it shows that we have cooked, smiled, fucked throughout the years not because it was easier for us than for anybody else, but because we did not have any other choice. Our faces have become distorted from so much smiling, our feelings have got lost from so much loving, our oversexualization has left us completely desexualized.

Wages for housework is only the beginning, but its message is clear: *from now on they have to pay us because as females we do not guarantee anything any longer.*[54]

The radical alternatives are hard to specify because any radical alternative involves the renegotiation of gender: a change in the social construction of the natural. Men become more nurturing; women become more independent, aggressive. The Parsonian division of labour breaks down. Can we then have a new kind of family? Or will we all then have to forgo that special kind of haven, that cell of culture, that personalized setting?

The radical outburst quoted just above may appear as a sharp contrast to, as an exception from the extraordinary conservatism of the prevailing division of labour within the household. But both the traditionalism of housework and the radical response to housework may be understood as stemming from the *same* peculiar characteristics of this 'most singular of occupations'. It is hard to bargain about the natural. To change housework seems to involve a repudiation of roles, a breaking with established social ties, the abandonment of personal commitments. It is not at all like claiming in union negotiations; and to place the division of labour in the household in a negotiating framework is at once to propose the most radical of changes in the social order and framework of claiming.

Similarly, in the world of work, as we show in the next chapter, claiming involving equal pay for equal work, while involving substantial social struggle, is, nevertheless, relatively established compared to the now asserted principle of 'equal pay for work of equal value'. Here women's claims encounter the natural in the form of the structure of occupations, an economic phenomenon grounded in implicit understandings as to women's natural capacities and appropriate social roles; these understandings are, as we have suggested, interrelated with the social conventions surrounding women's domestic role.

When we look at the women's movement in Chapter 6 we will see again how the intractability of explicit claiming in the realm of the natural came to divide the women's movement into a branch dealing with women's rights and one focused on women's liberation: and to lead to a number of very loosely linked intellectual trends in various fields to redefine the natural. These, we have argued, are not exactly claiming, but an indispensable basis for changing the ground rules so that certain sorts of claims, formerly rendered out of order, can be made.

NOTES

[1] Martin Murphy, 'Value of Household Work by Method of Valuation for the Noninstitutional Population 6 Years and Older', Bureau of Economic Analysis (mimeo), 1981.
[2] Ann Oakley, *The Sociology of Housework*, New York: Pantheon Books, 1974, p. 1.
[3] Joseph H. Pleck and Michael Rustad, 'Husbands' and Wives' Time in Family Work and Paid Work in the 1975-76 Study of Time Use', Working Paper No. 63, Wellesley College Center for Research on Women, 1980.
[4] Susan M. Strasser, 'An Enlarged Human Existence? Technology and Household Work in Nineteenth-Century America', in *Women and Household Labor*, ed. Sarah Fenstermaker Berk, Beverly Hills: Sage Publications, 1980, p. 37.
[5] Ibid., pp. 30-1.
[6] John P. Robinson, 'Housework, Technology and Household Work', in Berk, 1980, p. 54.
[7] Ibid., p. 63.
[8] Oakley, 1974, p. 112.
[9] Theodore Caplow, *The Sociology of Work*, New York: McGraw-Hill, 1954, p. 260.
[10] Ibid., p. 266.
[11] Monrad G. Paulsen, 'Support Rights and Duties between Husband and Wife', *Vanderbilt Law Review*, 9, 1956, pp. 709-42.
[12] Leonore J. Wietzman, 'Legal Regulation of Marriage: Tradition and Change: A Proposal for Individual Contracts and Contracts in Lieu of Marriage', *California Law Review*, 62, 1974, p. 1187. Quoted in Weitzman citation is *Rucci* v. *Rucci*, 23 Conn. Supp. 221, 224, 181, d 125, 127 (Super Ct. 1962).
[13] Cicely Hamilton, *Marriage as a Trade* (copyright 1909), London: The Women's Press Limited, 1981.
[14] Carol S. Bruch, 'Property Rights of De Facto Spouses Including Thoughts on the Value of Homemakers' Service', *Family Law Quarterly*, x:1, 1976, 101-36.
[15] Herma Hill Kay and Carol Amyx, 'Marvin vs. Marvin: Preserving the Options', *California Law Review*, 65, 1977, 937-79.
[16] Weitzman, p. 1189.
[17] Paulsen, pp. 712-13.
[18] Linda J. Beckman and Betsy Bosak Houser, 'The More You Have, The More You Do: the Relationship Between Wife's Employment, Sex-rule Attitudes and Household Behavior', *Psychology of Women Quarterly*, 4(2) (Winter 1979): 160-74; Julia A. Eriksen. William L. Yancey, and Eugene P. Eriksen, 'The Division of Family Roles', *Journal of Marriage and the Family*, 41 (2) (May 1979): 301-13; Dair Gillespie, 'Who has the Power? The Marital Struggle', *Journal of Marriage and the Family*, 33 (August 1971): 445-58; Maximiliane E. Szinovacz, 'Role Allocation, Family Structure, and Female Employment', *Journal of*

Marriage and the Family (November 1977): 781-91; Kathy Weingarten, 'The Employment Pattern of Professional Couples and their Distribution of Involvement in the Family', *Psychology of Women Quarterly*, 3 (1) (Fall 1978).

[19] Joseph Pleck, 'The Work-Family Role System', *Social Problems*, 24 (1977): 417-27.

[20] Maggie Schmitt, 'Female Employment and Women's Family Role', unpublished (23 January 1981).

[21] Ann Oakley, 'Reflections on the Study of Household Labor', in Berk, 1980.

[22] Chiara Saraceno (ed.), *Il lavoro mal diviso Ricerca sulla distribuzione dei carichi di lavoro nele famiglie*, Bari De Donato, pp. 37-8.

[23] Margaret Benston, 'The Political Economy of Women's Liberation', *Monthly Review* (1969), reprinted in Ellen Malos, *The Politics of Housework*, London: Allison and Busby, 1980.

[24] Eli Zaretsky, *Capitalism, The Family and Personal Life*, New York: Harper and Row, 1976, pp. 24-5.

[25] Ibid., p. 27.

[26] Ibid., pp. 28-9.

[27] Ibid., p. 31.

[28] Talcott Parsons and Robert F. Bales, *Family: Socialization and Interaction Process*, London: Routledge and Kegan Paul, 1956.

[29] Caplow, p. 268.

[30] Robinson, op. cit.; Wanda Minge-Klevana, 'Does Labor Time Decrease with Industrialization? A Survey of Time-Allocation Studies', *Current Anthropology*, 21, No. 3, 1980, pp. 279-87.

[31] Philippe Aries, *Centuries of Childhood: A Social History of Family Life*, New York: Vintage Books, 1962, p. 142.

[32] Ibid., p. 404.

[33] Carl N. Degler, *At Odds: Women and the Family in America from the Revolution to the Present*, New York: Oxford University Press, 1980.

[34] Ibid., p. 84.

[35] Sheila Robotham, *Woman's Consciousness, Man's World*, Harmondsworth: Penguin, 1973.

[36] With the conspicuous exception of Mary Douglas and Baron Isherwood *The World of Goods*, New York: Basic Books, 1979.

[37] Thorstein Veblen, *The Theory of the Leisure Class: An Economic Study of Institutions*, New York: Vanguard Press, 1912.

[38] William H. Whyte, *The Organization Man*, New York: Simon and Schuster, 1956.

[39] Baker Brownell, *Art Is Action: A discussion of nine arts in a modern world*, New York: Harper, 1939.

[40] Douglas and Isherwood, p. 119.

[41] James Ault, *Network Structure and the Practical Burdens of Housework and Child Care: Class Differences in Family Structure and the Social Bases of Modern Feminism*, (unpublished dissertation) Sociology Dept., Brandeis University, 1981.

[42] Richard A. Berk, 'The New Home Economics: An Agenda for Sociological Research', in Sarah Fenstermaker Berk, 1980, p. 134.

[43] See Berk, Sarah F. (ed.), *Women and Household Labor*, Sage Publications, 1980.
[44] Gary S. Becker, 'A Theory of Marriage: The Economics of the Family', in *The Economic Approach to Human Behavior*, Chicago: University of Chicago Press, 1976.
[45] Edward Shorter, *The Making of the Modern Family*, Fontana/Collins, 1975.
[46] Degler, 1980.
[47] Nancy Chodorow, *The Reproduction of Mothering: Psychoanalysis and the Sociology of Gender*, Berkeley: University of California Press, 1978.
[48] Alva Myrdal and Viola Klein, *Women's Two Roles: Home and Work*, London: Routledge and Kegan Paul, 1956, p. 143.
[49] Ann Oakley, *Woman's Work: The Housewife, Past and Present*, New York: Vintage Books, 1976.
[50] Briggs, 'Guess Who Has the Most Complex Job?' in Barbara Allen Babcock, Ann E. Freedman, Eleanor Holmes Norton, and Susan C. Ross, *Sex Discrimination and the Law: Causes and Remedies*, Boston: Little, Brown and Co., 1975, p. 204.
[51] Dolores Hayden, *The Grand Domestic Revolution*, Cambridge: MIT Press, 1981.
[52] David G. Gil, *Unravelling Social Policy: Theory, Analysis and Political Action towards Social Equality*, Cambridge: Schenkman Publishing Co., 1973.
[53] Ellen Malos (ed.), *The Politics of Housework*, London: Allison and Busby, 1980.
[54] Silvia Federici, 'Wages against Housework', in Ellen Malos (ed.), *The Politics of Housework*, 1980, pp. 257-8.

CHAPTER 4

Women and Work: The Incomplete Revolution

ONE of the dramatic developments in twentieth-century industrial society is the revolution in the labour-force participation of women. Women, of course, have always worked, but as men moved into the paid labour market women tended to remain in what became defined as the contrasting 'domestic sphere'. However, in the United States after 1900 about 20 per cent of women fourteen years of age and over were in the paid labour force. This meant that 18.1 per cent of the total labour force were women. These percentages increased very little in the next forty years. The tight labour market of the war years brought women into the labour force: from 1940 to 1945 women's participation increased from a little more than a quarter of the total labour force (25.4 per cent) to a little more than a third (35.7 per cent). At the end of the war, the percentage declined slightly. But then it began to go up again[1]. In other countries we find a similar pattern. By the late 1970s in the United Kingdom approximately 51 per cent of women 16 to 64 years of age are gainfully employed. In Sweden the rates are even higher, two-thirds of women being in the labour force.[2]

Growth in the female labour force has occurred slowly in the post-World War I period at a rate of about 1.5 per cent a year in the United States. Hence the impact of this revolution has largely gone unnoticed. It has been to use the title of a recent book on this subject, a Subtle Revolution.[3] In the meantime, while women's labour-force participation has increased since the 1950s, the overall economic activity rates of men have declined.

One of the implications of the increasing participation of women and reduced participation of men is that the composition of the total labour force has also changed. In 1980 in the United States women comprised about 42 per cent of the total labour force, up from 36 per cent in 1970 and 29 per cent in 1950.[4] Women's share in the labour force in Sweden is well over 42 per cent.

Extrapolating these trends would suggest that by the end of the century the Western industrial societies will have achieved sexual equity in participation rates, with Sweden leading the way. Of course not all countries are at this stage of development. The average female share of the labour force for all OECD countries was 35 per cent in 1976[5]. But if we assume that Sweden and the United States are lead countries, and that industrial societies tend to display similar patterns over time then we might expect that the other European countries will follow soon.

How shall we think about these developments in a claims framework?

One theme is obvious: the claims for equity which women make in the world of work. Whatever the part played by market demand — jobs which came into existence, and for which women seemed the available labour supply — the movement of women into wage labour has also involved claims by women to roles and rewards previously monopolized by men. The demands for entry into jobs which had been reserved to males; for affirmative action to redress the consequences of past barriers to entry; for equal pay — these are a large element in the movement for women's rights in recent years. Some of the processes by which these claims came into being, and the institutional responses to them, are summarized in a following chapter. In this part of the women and work story, women's claims are similar to those of other disadvantaged groups.

But women's claims have in other ways a very different character because of the fact that discussions of 'working women' implicitly treat women, especially wives and mothers, who are in the paid labour force as straddling two potentially conflicting realms of participation and claiming. From the standpoint of the family, we ask, for example; Can working mothers do justice to child-rearing? Or, from the standpoint of work, we ask; What occupations are best for women? or Are there bona-fide occupational qualifications which exclude women from certain jobs? Again, thinking about the interaction between two realms, we consider: Should husbands take more responsibility for housework? or Can the development of part-time work reduce the demands on working women?

Thus the topic of women and work not only raises questions as to women's claims within work, but also as to the consequences of women's work-force participation for family roles and for the structure of power within the family.

The conflict between work and family obligation is a new issue, because of a dramatic change in the category of women who work. By and large, the participation of young women (daughters), both those living at home and those forming their own households, has actually declined in most industrial societies, largely because more young women are continuing their education. (More recently, there has been a reversal of this pattern as young women have pursued both work and education either simultaneously or serially over the years.) The participation rates of women who have headed their own families have always been high and in recent years have increased only slightly. The participatory revolution is not a revolution of single women or of female heads. Rather, it represents a dramatic change in the labour-force-participation behaviour of wives in general and mothers in particular. In the first half of this century, the proportion of wives in the United States labour force increased from around five per cent to almost a quarter. In the next quarter of a century the proportion increased to nearly one-half for all wives. This amounts to a reasonably steady three per cent annual increase.

Of these changes in women's labour-force participation the most important appear to us to be in the participation of women who are also mothers of young children. One reason is that it is here that we see the sharpest increase. In the United States in 1978 the participation rate of married women living with their husbands and with children under three years of age reached an unprecedented 37.6 per cent, for women with children aged three to five years of age the rate was even higher, 47.0 per cent. In Sweden, which probably has a higher proportion of women in the paid labour force than any other country, the participation rate of married women with young children under seven was 51 per cent in 1975 compared with 22 per cent in 1965.[6]

We see these changes as important to the claiming story not merely because of the sharp increases in participation rates, but also because it is the group of working mothers which has the greatest potential, we should suppose, for changing the structure of claiming within the realm of the family; it is here that women's paid labour outside the home has the greatest likelihood of conflicting with traditional commitments to the 'domestic sphere'. Here we must distinguish two groups of working mothers: those who are married, and those who are the solo heads of families. There is a potential for role conflict in both cases, but this potential must play itself out differently in the two situations, depending on the claiming options available to women under different claims systems. The solo mother relies upon the state or she works, or some combination of both. However, choice between these options is by no means simply determined by the level of state provision. Sweden, which has a very high level of state provision, also has a very high level of labour-force participation. Claiming is not simply an economic calculus of demands and trade-offs but involves the structure of role expectations and value behaviour. In Sweden, women, including solo mothers, are expected to work and they do; in Britain, they were not expected to work and a larger proportion than in Sweden rely upon welfare. In the United States there was much more ambivalence about letting women rely upon welfare. While two-thirds of solo mothers receive welfare payments, public policy is committed to encouraging welfare mothers to work.

Some reformers and scholars have argued that the development of women's claiming in the economic realm through their increased labour-force participation is bound to produce in short order a change in women's claiming in the family realm. This theory has been called in a report by OECD 'the theory of the two revolutions'[7] but has also under other phraseology been put forward by the Urban Institute in the United States and in other sources.

The argument in the theory of the two revolutions can be summarized as follows.

This revolution in women's labour-force participation signals an equity revolution. It will make for a major and permanent change in the nature of the family as a social organization with repercussions not only for women's roles and identities, but also for the roles, identities, and life experiences of men and children. The equity revolution will involve:

(a) the differentiation of life-styles where marriage and child-rearing is not the only acceptable way for women to live a meaningful life, and

(b) relational equity, with women having a larger share in the exercise of power, authority, and decision-making within the nuclear family.

The State's social policies will serve as the handmaidens of these deep changes in the fabric of industrial society, both reflecting and leading these changes, through specific policies such as equal pay regulations, the expansion of child care, tax reform, and the redefinition of economic dependency leading towards individual rather than family income-support benefits.

We must agree with the 'two revolutions' theory in some part. As we have argued earlier, claiming in the three realms comprises a unified claims system, and changes in one realm must bring about a change in others. However, we see the changes in women's claiming in the realm of work as less far-reaching than the 'two revolutions' theory proposes. A first point is that the changes are less far-reaching than the theory proposes, because the theory assumes that claiming based on work depends solely on participation. To focus on participation is to ignore two other dimensions of the economic realm: long-term attachment to work, and the level of financial reward, which is translated into contribution to the family's resources. The two revolutions theory implicitly assumes that participation, attachment, and contribution are much more closely tied in the case of women than is in fact the case.

In addition, when we turn our attention to the distinction between participation, attachment, and contribution we see that from a feminist perspective there are serious problems of terminology. In discussing women and work, it turns out that we lack an adequate language for the discussion of the interaction between the realm of family and the realm of work.

A central issue which we shall be discussing is women's labour-force attachment. The argument as to whether women are able to claim for paid-work rewards equal to those of men has as its reciprocal the argument as to whether women work with the same degree of commitment that men do; do they tend to work full time within a year as much as men, and is their turnover from year to year roughly equivalent?

But the use of this language to describe attachment inhibits our understanding of reality. We describe people's behaviour in the labour market in terms of their actions — women are actively seeking full or part-time work. We speak of the demand for women's work and the segmented structure of female labour markets. We do not have a vocabulary to describe the joint behaviour of the interaction between people and the occupational structure. Attachment to work must be understood as a reciprocal relationship between the worker and her job. We can think of the nature of work attachment from two perspectives — as a job designed for turnover and replacement, or as part-time work. From the first perspective we are describing the characteristics of the job, from the second perspective the nature of the worker. We are thus trapped. We mean to describe the former, but we only have data for discussing the latter and we lack the vocabulary (that is, conceptual framework) for discussing the interaction between both. The reason that terminological issues are important is because they lie at the centre of the substantive issues, which have to do with the interaction between the structuring of women's personal commitments, the structure of the jobs available to women, and the structure of aspirations and commitments women make on their own behalf. What we call attachment is the more complex interaction between women and jobs. What we call contribution is the economic outcome of that interaction in both monetized and non-monetized forms. This requires a double transformation in the jobs available for women and in the way in which women work (that is, priority given to paid employment and to the deployment of energy and time in the household).

The terminological issues are important to us also because in struggling with them we find that we are encountering certain underlying definitions of the natural. The terminological problems involve incompatibilities between what seems natural in the realm of the economic and what seems natural in the personal or family realm. We shall return to this point later.

These limitations must be understood in the context of the discussion which follows.

Women's work will be important to women themselves, to their families, and to society generally if it is substantial and permanent rather than temporary. A first approach to understanding attachment is to examine the extent to which women work full or part time; the extent to which they work full time and full year; and the number of continuous years in the labour force. Each of these measures of attachment yields different insights into the phenomena. The most complete information we have on this questions comes from United States data based on the annual average of the monthly Current Population Surveys. In 1966, 26.4 per cent of employed women worked part time. This figure rose by 8.4 per cent and was 34.8 per cent in 1980. Although men's part-time work increased more rapidly than that of women, men started at a lower rate so only 11.5 per cent of men worked part time in 1980.[8]

But these figures only capture the pattern of work at a moment in time. When we examine whether women work all year round or simply on an intermittent or seasonal basis throughout the year, we get a very different picture. When we focus on women 25 to 54 years of age we find that less than half of those who worked were year-round full-time workers. The participation rate of women in this age group is about 60 per cent. This means therefore that only about one-third of all women aged 25 to 54 years were year-round full-time workers in 1977.[9]

If an attachment revolution has begun, it has a long way to go since two-thirds of the 25- to 54-year-old women were not fully employed by this broader definition.

An examination of trends by age suggests the beginnings of an attachment revolution. Between 1960 and 1977 the largest increase in year-round full-time employment occurred among women 24 to 35 years of age, where the proportion with year-round attachment almost doubled over the seventeen-year period, increasing from about 17 per cent to 33 per cent. When we examine the work behaviour of married women with children we find that full-time full-year attachment to work is low, ranging from 10 per cent for mothers with children under the age of three, to 16 per cent for mothers with children three to five years of age, to 26 per cent for those with school-age children. However, in all of these situations, there has also been a steady and continuous increase in work attachment since 1960.[10]

Taken together these data suggest that there has been a gradually increasing attachment to the labour force among women which can be detected for all groups whether based on age, marital status, or the ages of children. However, most of the increased labour-force participation of women who are mothers and wives is accounted for by the growth of part-time and part-year work. It appears that wives continue to adjust their work lives to the demands of home and children. Claiming in the world of work is still secondary to commitments to the domestic realm. Year-round full-time workers are becoming a larger proportion of all age groups. This is particularly true among young women. Nevertheless, attachment is clearly not keeping pace with the participatory revolution. The more rigorous the measure of attachment, the more we find a divorce between participation and continuous work attachment.

A similar pattern exists in Europe. The European Community Survey allows us to characterize women as full-time workers in the northern EEC countries of Germany, the children two-thirds of the employed women were part-time workers in the norther EEC countries of Germany, the United Kingdom, and Denmark. Interestingly enough, in the southern countries of France and Italy, while fewer women worked, only 20 per cent of those who did work were part-time workers. However data in the southern countries have to be interpreted cautiously because of 'hidden employment' — women working part-time but not reporting their earnings.

While from some perspectives, the pattern of part-time and intermittent work might be seen as a solution to the problem of competing claims spheres, it may also be seen as a way of getting the worst of both worlds. The wife/mother retains primary responsibility for the household, while working at jobs with relatively low pay, low job security, few fringes, and low opportunity for career mobility. As firms adjust their employment policy to a labour force looking for part-time work, they may find it very much to their advantage to have a reserve they can call on at their convenience — for example, at times of peak demand. If

Women and Work: The Incomplete Revolution

such a pattern develops, part-time work may accommodate much more to the needs of employers than to the needs of mothers.

A proper accounting of the wife's contribution to the household economy requires 'cashing out' the value of non-monetized services. Here again we confront the unresolved conceptual and methodological problems which imprison analysis in an intellectual framework which gives a greater reality to the market and, since the market is dominated by men, implicitly to the activities of men.

Nevertheless, we live in a society where the cash contribution is perceived as having a special standing in defining economic position. Knowing this to be only part of the story, let us examine the more restricted financial contribution of wives' employment to family income.

Potentially, changes in women's work and earnings (equal pay) could transform the income and life-style patterns among different types of households. But the findings in the United States suggest that working wives' contributions are low. An analysis of trends over time between 1960 and 1977 shows, quite surprisingly, that the proportion of family income that wives contribute in two-worker families has hardly changed. (See footnote 10.)

The pattern can be shown by citing the evidence from a recent comparative study of the sources of family income around 1970. (The years varied somewhat for each country.) Working married mothers contribute 22 per cent of family income[12] in the United States, 18 per cent in the United Kingdom, and 21 per cent in Sweden. On average, wives contribute about 30 per cent to family income and mothers about a fifth — somewhat more in Sweden and the United Kingdom. The proportion of wives that contribute more or less equally with men to the income of the family is very small. In the United States, only 5 per cent of the wives who were also mothers contributed as much as 40 per cent of the family income.

But the figures become even more dramatic and disturbing when we combine both attachment and contribution. The data for the period from 1968 to 1975 in the United States for women married for ten years indicate that only 7 per cent of the wives contributed more than 20 per cent of total family income in all ten years; and only 2.1 per cent contributed 33 per cent or more in every year of the ten-year period.

These figures do not, however, mean that wives' earnings are unimportant to the family. In the United States without the wives' earnings, about 9.5 per cent of working-wife families without children and about 16.4 per cent of families with children would have been poor. When the wives' income is included, the figures change dramatically. Among working-wife couples with no children the proportion defined as poor falls from 9.5 per cent to 1.2 per cent, and among working wives with children, the proportion declines from 16.7 per cent to 5.9 per cent. This suggests that of families which without the wife's earnings would have been in poverty, 88 per cent of the families without children and 52 per cent of those with children were moved out of poverty by the wives' earnings. A similar pattern exists for living standards other than that of poverty.

Indeed, Bob Gregory[13] has shown that in Australia it is becoming increasingly difficult to be included among the top family-income groups on the basis of a single family income.

Having made the case for the importance of wives' earnings, it would be a mistake to overstate the effect on the family of these earnings. We know from qualitative studies which we have carried out that in general a wife's earnings are not built into the family's basic standard of living as reflected in the choice of neighbourhood, of housing, and decisions about children's education unless the wife is defined as more or less steadily in the labour market. The data we have reported above refer only to the effect of a wife's earnings on the family income for one given year. We do not know whether the wife continues to work to keep the family out of poverty year in and year out. It is only when the wife works steadily that the family seems likely to 'live up to' the wife's income. In other words, unless the wife's contribution to the family income is continuous and stable over time, it is unlikely to influence the family's level of living significantly. Thus, even if a family is moved out of poverty by the wife's earnings, the family may nevertheless continue to consume at or close to the poverty level unless the family feels it can rely upon the wife's earnings over time. By and large, therefore, the wife's earnings are likely to have a small impact on the general consumption standards of those in poverty.

We may need to temper these conclusions in the light of further study. We need to know in much greater detail how the earnings of the wife get translated into changes in the family's life circumstances. This requires a study of the pooling of resources. We need to develop a sociology of household expenditures which examines and develops an understanding of the social meaning of items of consumption and investment.

A second way in which the earnings of married women are important is that they have an effect on their future economic situation should the marriage dissolve. In the United States it seems likely that well over a third of mothers will spend some time in the future as solo heads of their families. One study has shown that to the extent that wives become more regular labour-force participants, they increase the probability of having a stable and somewhat higher income situation should they become heads of their own families. In the fourth year that they headed their own family, women who had had regular work experience before becoming female heads had family incomes equal to 80 per cent of their average family income while a wife. In sharp contrast, women who had never worked at all had incomes slightly less than half that of their last married years.[14]

Accounting for the Interaction Between Family Claims and Work Claims

When most people ask why wives and mothers work, they assume that the reasons must be related to the household's economics. Two answers seem plausible, one implying a positive relationship, the other a negative relationship to the husband's economic position. In the negative case, the husband finds himself unable to work or earning very little. His wife enters the labour market in order to compensate for the husband's weak earning position. This is essentially a 'necessity-driven' image. The evidence that wives move families out of relative economic poverty suggests that economic necessity underlies the labour-force participation of some.

There is also a positive relationship between women's working and the family economy. Middle-class husbands are more likely than their working-class counterparts to encourage their wives to work and are less threatened by their activity in the labour market. The higher the husband's earnings the more likely is the wife to work. Part of this trend may be attributed to highly educated wives marrying highly educated husbands. The more highly educated wife faces a more favourable job market and hence the opportunity cost of remaining at home for her is high. This we could label the 'opportunity driven' model.

There is some empirical evidence in the United States which makes this model seem very plausible. When both the age and level of educational achievement are taken into account, better educated women seem more likely to work than less well educated women.

Among women 20 to 24 years of age we find the following: 48 per cent of women with eight years of basic education work, whereas 69 per cent work in the group that also has four years of high school, and of those who go to university for four years or more 88 per cent work.[15]

Rainwater and Rein's analysis of the association between wives' earnings and other components of the family income suggests that the models of 'necessity' and 'opportunity' both appear to be correct. Indeed, they appear to cancel each other out. It would not distort reality very much, to say that there is essentially no association between how much husbands earn, how much wives earn, and how much either or both of them earn, on the one hand, and how much other income is available to the family, on the other.

It is true that from an individual family's perspective these combinations certainly are not random. Each family has a history of a set of personal, social, and economic dynamics producing its particular family-income package of the employment and earnings of the husband, the wife, and other family members. Family structures change over time, as do individual motives for working and not working. Nevertheless, the overall pattern is one that does not differ very much from a model in which income components are combined in an almost random way. Thus, the association between the earnings of the husband and the wife could be explained by the way in which the conflicting pecuniary motives cancel each other out. However, we are sure that non-pecuniary motives are also at work.

It is as if, for many women, the money is almost a by-product of the even more important social and psychological gains from work and, therefore, is not essential to the choice of work. The finding of a very weak correlation between husband's and wife's employment and earnings is extremely suggestive of this conclusion.

To summarize the foregoing: We would expect that the participatory revolution by itself is unlikely to have a major effect on the reciprocal structuring of work claims and family claims. Participation is in itself not enough of a change in the realm of work to bring about the change within the family proposed by the 'two revolutions' theory. We would expect some reduction in housework, some assumption of tasks by husbands, some reduction, perhaps, in sleep and leisure time of wives, and perhaps some increase in the purchase of services to run the home. We might also expect to see some evidence of strain on families produced by time pressures, but no substantial renegotiation of the families' decision structure. We believe this to be true because the participatory revolution has not been accompanied by an attachment and contributory revolution. It is unlikely, therefore, that we will find any evidence for a significant move towards relational equity within the family.

A systematic review of the organization of family life comparing demographically similar one- and two-income-earner families would be needed to test this hypothesis. The evidence we have is partial and not wholly satisfactory; it suggests that some changes are going on, but the equity revolution does not seem to be here yet.

While one recent study has shown husbands of employed women increasing their share of child care, and while there is evidence for a decrease in domestic work by both empolyed and unemployed women,[16] there is no evidence of any substantial renegotiation of the division of domestic labour by gender. According to most studies, working wives continue to do most of the cooking, housework, and child care for their families. Several studies have shown that husbands of working wives do not spend significantly more time on housework and child care than husbands of non-working wives.

According to most studies, working wives continue to do most of the cooking, housework, and child care for their families. They do, however, spend less time on housework and child care than non-working wives do. A 1975 Urban Time-Use Study[17] found that in the United States working wives spend on average about twenty-five hours a week on 'family care' while non-working wives spend about forty-four hours. The difference seems to represent work foregone rather than work reallocated to other household members. Several studies have shown that husbands of working wives do not spend significantly more time on house and child care than husbands of non-working wives.

This is not to deny that there has been an important shift in the pattern of mutual expectation and sex roles. For example, we no longer see sex as a duty for the woman and as a benefit for the man. The 'sex role battle' has, by and large, now ended. However, the battle of the bedroom has now moved to the 'battle of the kitchen'.[18] Here, the question is who takes responsibility for keeping the house in order and for managing the housework and child care. It is here that the equity revolution has failed to take place. The male has stubbornly refused to budge. It is the woman's responsibility to organize the home. Men will help with tasks delegated to them by their wives. But the problem of the 'double day' (work at home and work in the market) persists because the working wife continues to carry the main psychological burden of managing and planning the distribution of time and tasks that must be carried out in the family. Even if she is relieved of some of the physical burdens of home production with the advent of modern technology and modern appliances, and even if the husband is willing to assume some specific household tasks, the responsibility still remains essentially hers. Men appear to be willing to take on recreational tasks of taking children to various places, but they have resisted the maintenance tasks of buying clothes, taking children to the dentist, and being responsible continuously for the preparation of meals. What men have consistently done is to reject the taking of full responsibility for domains in the home, such as child care, home cooking, and so on.

They are prepared to negotiate with their wives around specific tasks. And so we hear the refrain 'Tell me what to do and I'll do it'. Women have not helped, because they have refused to relinquish responsibilities for domains within the household.

There are two major transformations in women's roles, one involving the simultaneous participation by women, at least from time to time, in both child-rearing and work roles, and another, just now beginning, involving the deepening and intensification of work roles and identities. It is the minority of women who have already made this second transformation but there is evidence that it might happen in the future with more younger generation wives becoming more continuously attached to work and making significant contributions to family income. If this continues to happen, the next decades may see quite dramatic and important shifts in the life-course pattern of women and in relational equity in the families in which they live. Younger cohorts born after the 1940s appear to be establishing, in their twenties and thirties, patterns of delayed marriage, higher household headship, lower fertility, and higher divorce rates. These women may not be 'settling down' in marriage and parenting as fast as earlier cohorts, if at all; they may be developing life-styles characterized by less permanency and less attachment to the conventional pattern of nuclear-family living. Within the nuclear family these women will insist on relational equity and they will call for changes in domain responsibilities and not merely task-sharing.

Here a new issue must be brought forward. We have discussed attachment and contribution as though they were closely linked; women's contribution to family income closely reflect her continuity of work experience.

At one level, this relationship is obvious. The more years of work, and the more those years are ones of full-time employment, the more must be aggregate earnings. But we ordinarily think of the relationship between attachment and earnings as involving a deeper level of causality. Steady, full-time employment should lead to the acquisition of skills and the development of responsibility in the work organization which should be, in turn, rewarded by higher earnings. The difference between the primary and the secondary labour market is thought of as one in which rapid turnover and low earnings are linked; the 'bad jobs' of the labour-intensive, low-wage forms are designed for rapid turnover and ready replacement from a pool of relatively undifferentiated workers. We may well imagine that as women move in and out of the labour market to adapt to domestic responsibilities, or seek out part-time employment, they may well expect to receive relatively low per-hour wages. Thus, a relatively low level of income contribution may be interpreted as a natural consequence of weak labour-force attachment.

There is more to it than that, however. A recent attempt to investigate the extent to which differences in work history, on-the-job training, absenteeism, and self-imposed restrictions on work hours and locations accounted for wage differences between the sexes and races casts substantial doubt on this proposition. While differences in completed on-the-job training accounted for 11 per cent of the wage-gap between white men and white women, and difference in the proportion of full-time work accounted for 8 per cent, 'the large average difference in years spent out of the labour force since school completion (ranging from 3.5 to 5.2 years) explained little of the average wage gap between white men and black women'.[19]

Women's lower earnings, and therefore, lesser contribution to household income, must therefore be explained in another way — presumably in the peculiarities of the occupational structure which differentiate 'men's jobs' from 'women's jobs', and attach substantially lower wages to the latter.

In this interaction between the claiming spheres of the work realm and the domestic realm the realm of the State also has a part to play, on which we will comment in a subsequent chapter.

One might expect that lower earning potential would in itself lead to a lesser attachment to the labour force on the part of women compared to men. Thus the interaction between family-claims system and work-claims system is such that all three revolutions — participation, attachment, and contribution — are linked.

The Limits of the Natural

Proponents of the theory of two revolutions fail to recognize the structural obstacles to relational equity. They fail to take account of the implicit understandings of femininity and family structure which limit women's commitment to the world of work, and of the division of labour and patterns of remuneration which limit their contribution to family income — the arrangements which we have lumped together as included in the conventionalized 'natural'. The outcome of these factors is to limit the consequences of participation itself. The claiming story is more than the particular claims which women make in each domain (Men should help with housework; Equal Pay for Equal Work) but also involves a continual subtle readjustment of the *implicit* claims which are implied by the ideas of the nature of things — within both the constitution and functioning of the family and the occupational division of labour, and in the way the State interacts with both.

From time to time, explicit claiming erupts with reference to the 'natural' arrangements within these realms. Zaretsky[20] treats the family as an institution in the political economy of capitalism; feminist psychology questions the 'naturalness' of femininity and the 'maternal instinct'; lawyers connected with the Equal Opportunity Commission refuse to take for granted the 'men's jobs' and 'women's jobs' and ladders for internal promotion of a large corporation. But a good deal of the claiming which goes on around women's work takes place almost invisibly in the definition and redefinition of the natural within both work and the family.

In the preceding chapter we have tried to call attention to different and reciprocal claims, commitments, interests, and skills within the family; it is not simply women's domestic labour and men's obligation to support that which is at stake, but deeply-rooted conceptions of the masculine and feminine. It is this pattern of reciprocity which is experienced as the natural. The result is that claims on women's work in the family and women's claims for support are experienced as aspects of social role, interpersonal ties, and individual character.

In the realm of work, the 'two revolutions' theory fails to take account of the nature of the occupational structure within which women make their claims. There are at least three salient characteristics of this structure. One is the high degree to which work is packaged into 'men's' and 'women's' jobs. In 1978 almost 70 per cent of employed women were in occupations which had a substantial over-representation of women; only 10 per cent were in predominantly male jobs, and 22 per cent were in integrated jobs.[21] There seems to be some recent reduction in gender segregation, but the pattern is still very marked. Second, we note that women are predominantly in occupations which require, or appear to require, less skill and receive less pay than those of men. Between 1940 and 1970 women tended more than men to move into occupations 'characterized by low complexity, low autonomy, high supervision, low training and educational requirements, and low pay'.[22] In addition to asking whether women necessarily must occupy such jobs, we may also question the nature of the standards of classification themselves. These standards come from an elaborate system of classification developed by the Department of Labor which, as discussed in the previous chapter, assumes that the kind of work in which women tend to be employed requires very little skill. Third, women in general earn less than men. In the first place, women are more likely than men to work part time or when they work full time to work fewer hours than men. In addition, women tend to earn less per hour. In May 1978 the usual weekly earnings of women working full time were 61 per cent that of men also working full time. This proportion was somewhat lower than it was in May 1967 when the proportion was 63 per cent.[23]

In the realm of the State, the theory fails to take account of the deep ambivalence concerning the desirability of pursuing policies which may lead to changes in life-styles having as their consequence a decrease in fertility, an increase in mother-headed families, and a displacement of young and older workers. While there is considerable controversy about the degree to which women displace other workers, it appears clear that the mere surfacing of the questions of displacement and alternative life-styles leads to uncertainty and controversy, with the result that the government fails to develop a coherent policy about women's work. In this context, family policy runs the risk of becoming a code word for a regressive action designed to keep women in the home. Such a 'tacit policy' inhibits relational equity between the sexes, and avoids a coherent policy which accepts the implications that follow from women becoming full partners with men in the production of family money income.

The difficulty of arriving at a coherent policy, the muddled and conflicting measures which in fact emerge, reflect more than the usual conflict of interests. The difficulties also reflect the ambiguities of claim and counter-claim, and of the adjudication of conflicting claims, within areas which we think of as 'the natural', outside the normal sphere of policy intervention. We think that it is in theory possible to apply a claims framework to the entitlements and struggles for advantage within the areas socially defined as natural — but it is clear that a claims framework is applied there with some awkwardness.

One of the striking aspects of the women's movement of the sixties and seventies was the gradual press of explicit claiming into the natural realms of the family and the occupational structure, a set of intellectual and political developments which we can also describe as the redefinition of the boundaries of the natural. On the one hand, women's liberation groups called into question the naturalness of women's special role in the family, of traditional definitions of womanly character, of the family itself. On the other hand, feminist lawyers questioned the naturalness of only men doing electrical work and women being especially suitable as flight attendants on airplanes. The Equal Employment Opportunity Commission's summary of its case against Bell Telephone turned the company's evidence of women's weak labour-force attachment back against it by arguing that neither the company's organizational and occupational structure nor women's work behaviour in the company should be taken as natural; each should be understood as the reciprocal of the other. The statement argues:

Although women continue to be employed in very large numbers, they are confined to the most stifling and repetitive jobs. Their compensation is so meager as to make them doubt their own self worth. Their prospects for promotion are in the distant future, if at all. It is little wonder, therefore, that many women flee from telephone jobs almost as quickly as they are attracted to them.[24]

The consent decree negotiated with the telephone company

not only proposed changes in recruiting, but also substantial reorganization of the internal career ladders within the company so as to change the system of incentives confronting women workers. A situation which had been defined in terms of high turnover and weak labour-force attachment was given a new terminology of attraction, incentive, role models, and the building of a sense of self-worth.

NOTES

[1] June O'Neill and Rachel Braun, 'Women and the Labor Market, A Survey of Issues and Policies in the United States', Washington, DC: Urban Institute, 1981, p. 3.

[2] Martin Rein, 'Women and Work: The Incomplete Revolution', *The Australian Economic Review*, 3rd Quarter 1980, pp. 10–17.

[3] Ralph E. Smith (ed.), *The Subtle Revolution: Women at Work*, Washington DC: The Urban Institute, 1979.

[4] O'Neill, ibid.

[5] Organization for Economic Cooperation and Development (OECD), *Labor Force Statistics*, Paris, France, August 1981.

[6] Ibid.

[7] *The Equity Revolution*, Paris, France: OECD, 1978.

[8] Information on part-time work for women came from unpublished annual data prepared by the Department of Labor from the Current Population Survey.

[9] Lee Rainwater, Martin Rein, and Joseph Schwartz, *Family Income Packaging in Britain, Sweden and the United States* (forthcoming).

[10] George Masnick and Mary Jo Bane, *The Nation's Families 1960 to 1990*, an Outlook Report of the Harvard–MIT Joint Center for Urban Studies, June 1980, Cambridge, Mass.: Auburn House, 1981.

[11] Lee Rainwater, 'Mother's Contribution to Family Income in Europe and the United States', *Journal of Family History*, June 1979.

[12] Lee Rainwater, Martin Rein, and Joseph Schwartz, op. cit.

[13] Bob Gregory, 'The Relevance of Segmented Labor Market Theories: The Australian Experience of the Achievement of Equal Pay for Women', a paper presented to the Economic Society of Australia and New Zealand, August 1978. (Mr Gregory is at the Australian National University at Canberra.)

[14] Lee Rainwater, Martin Rein, and Joseph Schwartz, op. cit.

[15] O'Neill and Braun, op. cit.

[16] William Alonso, 'The Population factor in Urban Form', in Arthur Solomon (ed.), *Prospective Metropolis*, Boston, Mass: MIT Press, 1979.

[17] Joseph H. Pleck and Michael Rustad, 'Husbands and Wives Time in Family Work and Paid Work in the 1975–76 Study of Time Use', Working Paper No. 63, Wellesley College Center for Research on Women, 1980.

[18] These observations are based on discussion with Robert S. Weiss of the Harvard University Laboratory of Community Psychiatry. See also Robert S. Weiss, *Going it Alone*, New York: Basic Books, 1979.

[19] Mary Corcoran and Greg J. Duncan, 'Work History, Labor Force Attachment, and Earnings Differences Between the Races and Sexes', *Journal of Human Resources*, xiv: 1, pp. 3-20. and Richard A. Berk, 'Sex Earnings, and the Nature of Work: A Job-Level Analysis of Male-Female Income Differences', *Social Science Quarterly*, Vol. 58, No. 4, March 1978.

[20] Eli Zartetsky, *Capitalism, the Family, and Personal Life*, New York: Harper and Row, 1976.

[21] O'Neill and Braun, op. cit.

[22] Steven Dubnoff, 'Beyond Sex Typing: Capitalism, Patriarchy and the Growth of Female Employment 1940-1970', University of Michigan, Institute for Social Research, August 1978, pp. 14-15.

[23] Janice N. Hedges and Earl F. Mellor, 'Weekly and Hourly Earnings of U.S. Workers, 1967-78', *Monthly Labor Review*, August 1979, US Bureau of Labor Statistics.

[24] Barbara Allen Babcock, Ann E. Freedman, Eleanor Holmes Norton, Susan C. Ross, *Sex Discrimination and the Law: Causes and Remedies*, Boston: Little Brown and Company, 1975, p. 289.

CHAPTER 5

Women and the State

IN 1873, the statement made by Susan B. Anthony at her trial (and conviction) for voting draws a picture of a world in which the State and women are utterly distinct.

> Your denial of my citizen's right to vote is the denial of my right or consent as one of the governed, the denial of my right of representation as one of the taxed, the denial of my right to a trial by a jury of my peers as an offender against law .... All of my prosecutors, from the 8th ward corner grocery politician, who entered the complaint, to the United States Marshal, Commissioner, District Attorney, District Judge, your honor on the bench, not one is my peer, but each and all are my political sovereigns; and had your honor submitted my case to the jury, as was clearly your duty, even then I should have had just cause of protest, for not one of those men was my peer; but, native or foreign born, white or black, rich or poor, educated or ignorant, awake or asleep, sober or drunk, each and every man of them was my political superior; hence, in no sense, my peer ....
> Precisely as no disfranchised person is entitled to sit upon a jury, and no woman is entitled to the franchise, so, none but a regularly admitted lawyer is allowed to practice in the courts, and no woman can gain admission to the bar — hence, jury, judge, counsel, must all be of the superior class.[1]

The world which we confront a century later is quite different. Women are no longer so completely outside the State. Women vote, serve on juries, are admitted to the bar, hold public office. At the same time, the State has entered civil society in a variety of new ways. Modern social life is characterized both by the engagement of women in public life, and by a more publicly managed economy. The activities of the State have become so pervasive that it is a major undertaking simply to define the State and to map what it does, and a substantial research project to trace the consequences of these actions on the economic position of women.

The State regulates the labour market, imposing minimum wages, taxing payrolls, regulating the conditions of hiring, firing, promotion, and training and retirement. Through its power to tax firms and workers, the State creates a transfer system parallel to the distribution of wages. The State is both a purchaser from the private sector and a contractor to the private and non-profit sector. The order of magnitude is impressively large — in 1980, Federal purchases of goods and services was $199 billion out of total Federal expenditures of $601 billion.[2] The State is also a very large direct employer. So it is clear that while women have entered public life, the State has entered private life.

The relationship between women and the State is therefore extremely complex. We shall discuss this relationship in terms of three broad categories of State function: that of provider, that of regulator, and that of employer. In this analysis, the discussion of the State as employer will appear disproportionately large. This is simply because an extensive body of literature exists on the first two roles, while very little systematic work has been done on the State as employer, particularly with reference to its implications for women.

Government as Provider

Government as provider can rely on various alternative principles. The basic choice involves two conflicting ways of looking at the matter. One view — the contribution principle — limits the individual's access to support to what he or she has put in. This links to the operations of the market: having a job, contributing a part of one's wages, and having the employer match that contribution. (Of course, the employer can pay for it all, in which case the cash wages are likely to be lower.) In this case, the State, in its legislative, administrative, and legal roles, merely sets the rules for provision. The alternative principle of provision is based on some concept of collective solidarity. Here the State acts as a provider and support is not limited to contributions. Instead, support is collective and is based either on the principle of need or on common citizenship. American social policy has, by and large, relied upon need. The US does not have a universalistic family-allowance programme; there is an Aid to Families with Dependent Children programme, and an elaborate set of specialized means-tested programmes such as Medicaid, food stamps, general assistance, and Supplementary

Security income. In contrast, Continental social policy is more likely to rely upon principles of citizenship, with some countries like Britain struggling for a position between the two.

Which of the two general principles of provision — contribution or solidarity — is better for women? Both principles pose intractable problems for women, and either course of action taken by the state is vulnerable to criticism.

If we look at the way in which women fare in the contributory system by comparing their position relative to men *within the contributory system* we miss two fundamental issues: the relatively disadvantaged position of women within the labour market, on which the social-security system is based, and their non-monetized contribution within the domestic economy outside the labour market.

Danzinger et al.[3] have analysed the 1977 Current Population Survey and reported participation rates in social security, public assistance (AFDC, SSI, General Assistance), and other transfers (unemployment, workmen's compensation, government employees, and veteran's benefits). Their findings show that while women comprise 26 per cent of all household heads (including both single-person and multiple-person households), they account for 41 per cent of all social-security retirement recipients. Men, by contrast, account for 74 per cent of all households but only 59 per cent of all beneficiaries.

At the beginning of 1977 over sixteen million women were drawing some form of social security. Eight million women received benefits solely on the wage records of their husbands (3.4 million as the wives of retired or disabled workers, 4 million as elderly or disabled widows, and 0.6 million as young widowed mothers with children in their care). An additional 8.6 million women received benefits based on their own wage record. Twenty per cent of these workers (1.7 million) also received partial benefits as wives or widows. These figures show that 61 per cent of women beneficiaries make some claim for benefits based on their family rather than their work role.

If we compare only those women workers who actually make contributions, the outcome for women is still favourable; they have longer life expectancies; they are less likely to work beyond the age of sixty-five; and since they are more likely to have been in low-paying jobs, they receive a greater benefit from the weighted benefit formula. Robert Ball, former commissioner of Social Security, calculates that if . . . contribution rates were to cover the cost of cash benefits derived from the wage record of women, contributions would need to be one-fourth higher for women than for men.[4]

Female workers account for about 28 per cent of the total contributions received by the social-security system, but women draw 54 per cent of the total benefits from it.[5] (This is, of course, a consequence of the fact, to be discussed subsequently, that women derive their claims for entitlement in the social-security system both from their family and from their labour-market roles, and disproportionately from the former).

While a comparison of men and women shows women to hold a favourable position in some dimensions to that of men, on other dimensions the situation is quite different. As a consequence of the fact that women earn less than men in the labour market, even though the social-security benefits system is weighted towards low-wage workers, there remains a substantial gap between what men and women receive in the system. As of 1977, the average monthly benefits paid to men without reduction for early retirement amount to $308: for women with similar benefits, the average monthly sum was $215.[6]

Furthermore, the consequence of entitling women to make a claim based on family dependency via the social-security system is that working women are penalized versus housewives. A working woman, married to a working man, may find that years of payments into the social-security system entitles her household to receive very little more than it would if she had never worked and was now entitled to receive benefit as a dependant. This situation is a classic example of the problem of interaction between claims realms.

The difficulty has been that almost every remedy proposed implies another type of inequity from the one that already exists. To allow a married man the benefit payable to a couple while simultaneously paying his wife as a retiree clearly contradicts the notion of dependency. If the woman has earned income, and established her own rights to benefits, then she is not dependent. But to continue the present practice of simply making up the difference between a woman's benefit as a wife and her benefit as a retired worker means that the married woman has contributed a heavier tax rate than other women or than married men.[7]

Other features of women's labour-force participation also make for problems in the contributory system. 'Changing the requirements for disability benefits to require seven-and-one half years of work in the previous ten (up from five years at present) would screen out most women because they more frequently have interrupted employment because of child-bearing or rearing. Under the present law only about 40 per cent of women, compared to about 90 per cent of men, are covered by disability insurance. Nevertheless, in May 1980 women were almost half of all adult disabled beneficiaries — 16 per cent in their role as dependants and 33 per cent in their role as workers.[8]

If we look at the other benefits system which is closely tied to work, that is unemployment, workmen's compensation, and government-employee and veterans' benefits, women are clearly underrepresented. Here they comprise only 18.8 per cent of recipients.

In various ways, claims have been brought against the Social Security System to develop a system of regulations more favourable to women. In a contributory system, any group of people disadvantaged in the labour market will reflect that disadvantage in the benefit structure to some degree. The more one tries to compensate for the operations of the labour market, the more anomalies and inequities are produced which have the effect of undermining the rationale of the contributory logic of broadly relating contributions to benefits. It then appears necessary, if we are to avoid these anomalies, to deal directly with the occupational structure.

The Title VII case brought against AT&T constituted a test-case confrontation of the anomalies in the occupational structure which contribute to lower wages, weaker labour-force attachment, and shorter career ladders for women.[9] The AT&T case set an important legal precedent, but the practice did not spread, and by the 1980s the Court seemed to have backed away from this strong position. But the issue of equal pay for equal work and equal pay for work of equal value still smoulders and from time to time resurfaces in both the political and legal system. The outcome of this process is still indeterminate.

Meanwhile, a totally different way of approaching the question of equity for women in the social-security and other contributory systems is to introduce a claims rationale which argues for compensating women for the value of their indirect contribution to the co-production of family income. So far, however, development in this direction has not gone far, as the Supreme Court has rejected the claim on the capital resources of the family produced by the wife's efforts. The court argued that wives do not have access to the military pensions of their ex-husbands. These pensions are the 'personal entitlement, of the person who earned them, and may therefore not become part of the property settlement in divorce.[10] Nevertheless, it could be argued that the role of wives is different in the case of men employed in the military as compared with their civilian counterparts. Also we may observe the fact that some European countries do accept that women are co-producers of their husbands' income. The West German Supreme Court ruled that wives have a claim on their husbands' pensions and husbands a claim on their wives' pensions; thus the pension must be equally split. The cost of implementing this principle can be substantial, depending on how precisely the rule is interpreted. This question is not settled, but at least as far as Germany is concerned a political decision must be made by 1984.

In summary, the problem posed for women in the contributory system is that entitlement depends either on having a good job, or on having a grasp upon some man who does or did have one. For many women, neither condition prevails. Let us recall again that women who are supporting households are doing so in an economy in which women's full-time jobs pay on the average 59 per cent of men's. Women in this position must have recourse to the State based on some principle other than that of past contribution. In the American system, they can appeal only to the principle of need.

An elaborate system has been developed to define the standard of need and rules of eligibility and, increasingly, to specify the items of consumption for which government resources are directed; earmarked benefits have grown enormously with respect to unrestricted cash grants. In an industrial society governed by market principles, claims based on recognized economic contribution are held in much higher esteem ('You deserve it') than claims based on need ('You poor thing'). Needs programmes are legitimated by compassion, and the idea that success reflects merit easily relates compassion to contempt. Meanwhile, the level of provision must be below that at the low end of the wage structure, so as not to threaten dominant forms of claiming by undermining the incentive to work, and the necessary consequence is that recipients of needs programmes must live at a level below that of the conventional norms of consumption of society. There have been, historically, periods of relative liberality when anxiety about work incentives was reduced, and benefits became more generous relative to wages, but such periods do not appear to last, largely because the economic situation changes, and the political support by and on behalf of needy groups weakens. Once political support for the needy weakens, there are moves to 'tighten up' the system to eliminate fraud, abuse, and error. In these shifting climates of opinion, the recipients of aid are stigmatized by the new era of administrative stringency.

The stigmatizing and stingy character of needs-based programmes are inherent aspects of relying on the needs principle in a market-dominated society. These problems are clearly not specific to women. However, they affect women disproportionately, since women, being particularly disadvantaged in the contributory system, are more prone to falling into the needs programmes.

Not surprisingly, therefore, women find themselves disproportionately in the means-tested public-assistance system. In 1977, two-thirds of all families headed by young women with a child received Aid to Families with Dependent Children and women at all stages of the life cycle comprised 60 per cent of all public-assistance recipients.[11]

Government as Regulator

We use the term regulation to mean a broad spectrum of

activities through which government controls, or attempts to control, the activities of its citizens. We resist giving a restricted definition to the term regulation. We use the term broadly to include the activities of legislatures and courts, as well as those of the administrative bodies ordinarily designated as 'regulatory agencies', and we would like to be able to think about taxation, subsidies, and credit as forms of the State's regulation of the private sector. We mean by regulation generally what is ordinarily meant by the 'power of the State'. Regulation is the formal framework of the claims system, and constitutes the major way in which the State shapes the economic lives of women, aside from its role as a welfare provider, and as an employer.

We identify three regulatory realms: legislation, administration, and the courts. There is room for claiming in each realm, but each presents a different structure for claiming, and thus involves a different claiming process.

In the legislative arena we can identify two ways in which the law is used for women's claims. One is concerned with the realm of the symbolic, where statements of intention, even without much enforcement potential, are sought: the other is the more practical and strategic effort to exploit ambiguity in the law in the bid for more resources. A good example of the former is the struggle for the Equal Rights Amendment, a feminist project with a high degree of symbolic content. However, symbolic politics is risky. Persons both within and outside of the feminist movement have argued that other legislative, legal, or organizational strategies would produce greater gains for women with less potential for failure, and that failure runs the risk of producing loss of morale and political credibility for the women's movement. The constitutional amendment, if passed, does not prevent states from using gender as a category in the law; only that states be required to provide a justificatory rationale for such action. Nevertheless, the symbolic importance of affirming equal rights for women as a constitutional principle seemed to outweigh the costs and dangers of pursuing this strategy.

An example of resource-acquisition claiming is the field of child care where three groups having potentially conflicting interests were brought together: welfare, which was concerned with making it possible for women to work; child development, which was concerned with the compensatory education of children; the civil-rights groups which saw the programme as having potential for the exercise of decentralized political power.

The processes of claiming which take place in the legislative arena involve both bargaining and coalition-building within the legislative body and the mobilization of interest groups outside. The process of bargaining and coalition-building has special bearing on resource acquisition, while the process of mobilization has special bearing on the declaration of legislative intentionality, but both kinds of claiming, in fact, relate to each sort of legislative outcome: the more effective the mobilization, the better the capacity to bargain internally. On the other hand, the need to bargain and form coalitions internally makes demands on movement organization. Freeman's book on the politics of the women's movement is a discussion of precisely this sort of interaction.[12]

Administration is the realm of interpretation, which we associate especially with the writing of regulations and guide-lines, and of implementation, in which resources are translated into action. The relation between legislation and implementation in these two senses has received a great deal of attention. Although theorists of democracy may argue that there should be a unification of the two processes of legislation and administration, by following the principle of strict 'compliance', in practice a gap exists between the two, which leaves room for independent claiming in the realm of administration. This takes place on at least three different levels. The first is with respect to the interpretation of legislative intent in the form of specific regulation-writing. Historically, this was part of the arena of 'closed-door' politics, but with the mandating of the publication of guidelines in the Federal Register, this has become part of 'open-door' politics, and hence is a continuation of the legislative process; when new regulations are issued, mobilization is essential.

The second level is that of interpretation in the form of the personnel who man the regulatory and administrative agencies. One strategy in the use of the appointment process is a long delay in appointing anyone. The agency loses momentum and cannot defend its turf at that critical point of enthusiasm when a new administration comes into political power. An example would be the Reagan administration's delay in appointing a head for the Women's Bureau in the Department of Labor. When a previous administration created a new agency to defend some interest, a new administration less sympathetic to such an interest has three courses. Sometimes, of course, they can abolish the agency, as President Reagan, for example, abolished the President's Commission on the Status of Women. But when unable to take so drastic a course of action, an administration wishing to change policy may appoint someone hostile to the agency's founding mission. Again, the Reagan administration was able to express a general policy position towards limiting 'reproductive rights' by appointing persons with congenial views to head the Surgeon General's office and Department of Health and Human Services. Finally, they can understaff the agency and thus effectively destroy its capacity to act efficiently.

The third level of interpretation is at the level of access. There is always some element of discretion in the further interpretation of the rules of entitlement which determine an inividual's access to services, financial provision, credit, remission from taxes etc. This area of discretionary action takes place at the point where bureaucrat and citizen interact. Here ideas of professionalism and prevailing standards of operational practice govern.

Claims which seek to modify the interpretation of rules by personnel take two forms. One is the intellectual task of defining the proper exercise of professional discretion. In the Sixties, there was a vigorous debate in a number of professions around the issue of allegiance, with claiming taking the form of pushing for a shift of loyalty from bureaucracy or profession to consumer. This had consequences for women in many fields. For example, with respect to obstetrical practice it was argued that the degree of physical restraint on the delivery table, the automatic use of anaesthesia, and the barring of husbands from the delivery room were all practices developed for the convenience of doctors and hospital routines and should be altered to give women a greater degree of control over childbirth. Another debate about the nature of professional practice has been taking place with respect to conceptions of normality embedded in psychoanalytic practice with women/Feminists arguing that a profession historically dominated by males has used Freudian theory to rationalize a practice which tried to lead women clients into accepting a subordinate position in interpersonal relations and in society in general.

Quite a different process of claiming takes place at the level of mobilization in which the attempt is made to alter practice directly. Persons opposed to abortion have recently massed in groups before abortion clinics demonstratively asserting that the professionals in these clinics are involved in acts of murder, and aggressively arguing with clients of the services as they enter or leave. Political mobilization is used to alter practice both in the direction of feminist views and in the other direction as well.

In the courts, past precedent and immediate circumstances are joined via legal reasoning to produce a decision. The decision, with its reasoning, becomes a part of the regulatory structure. This process, encapsulated as it is, yet leaves room for claiming. Although it has been said, 'Let justice be done though the heavens fall', judges must inevitably in their decisions take into account what they deem to be prudent social policy. Furthermore, legal reasoning must inevitably draw on the conceptualizations of reality prevailing in society at a given point of time. For example, a decision by the Arizona Supreme Court in 1953, affirming the common-law rule that the domicile of the wife must follow that of the husband, offered as 'sound reasons' the following argument:

The law imposes upon the husband the burden and obligation of the support, maintenance and care of the family and almost of necessity he must have the right of choice of the *situs* of the home. There can be no decision by a majority rule as to where the family home shall be maintained, and a reasonable accompaniment of the imposition of the obligations is the right of selection. The violation of this principle tends to sacrifice the family unity, the entity upon which our civilization is built. The principle is not based on the common law theory of the merger of the personality of the wife with that of the husband; it is based on the theory that one domicile for the family home is still an essential way of life.

Although to the Arizona judge in 1953, this seemed self-evident, such reasoning appeared to a group of feminist lawyers in 1975 'in the light of modern day sociological and legal conditions, specious and unrealistic'.[13]

Although government has a broad arena for the exercise of regulation in the ways described above, and although claiming attempts to modify the regulatory role of government in each of these arenas, there are important limits to the regulatory role of government. These difficulties of enforcement constitute both a limit to claiming and another form of claiming.

There is a limit to what the agencies of the State can oversee. For example, if abortions are rendered illegal, it will still be possible for people to carry out abortions beyond the scrutiny of regulatory agencies and police. A change in the regulatory structure will therefore not eliminate abortions; it will change the way in which they are carried out. Thus there is a limit to the claiming of the anti-abortionists.

These limits of enforcement also become another form of claiming, in that, if the banned practices become widespread they produce a disjunction between rule and practice which may come to threaten the legitimacy of rules and the rule-making apparatus. As in the case of Prohibition, the State may give in on the particular to preserve its authority in general. Thus, individual rule violation may become a form of claiming.

Government as Employer

The State as provider and regulator gives rise to the role of the State as employer. Critics of the State from both ends of the political spectrum have observed that one of the side effects of carrying out the providing and regulating roles was the creation of a services bureaucracy to administer the programmes created by these tasks. Such criticism has taken the form of arguing that government is serving not so much the poor, as the service providers, or that it is creating a kind of 'new class' with an interest in promoting the expansion of government. Aside from these critiques, we explore in some detail the role of the state as employer since there has been little systematic review of women as employees of the State and the effects on the provider and regulator roles on the State's employer roles.

Let us begin with government as a direct employer, leaving until later government's role in creating employment indirectly via what we call the 'social welfare economy'.[14]

Between 1940 and 1980, employment in the public sector increased from 11.1 per cent to 19 per cent of the total civilian non-agricultural labour force. For women, the proportions are higher — 13.9 per cent in 1940 and 20 per cent in 1980.

Women workers are a steadily increasing part of the labour force, comprising more than half of the increase in the labour force in the past several decades. The expansion of jobs in government has been an important factor in this gradual increase in the employment of women.

In the post-war era, we can identify three periods of change in the employment contribution of the government sector.

(1) The first period occurred between 1940 and 1960 when government accounts for 12 per cent of the level of employment of women at the beginning of the period and 15 per cent at the end. Most of this increase occurred in the late 1950s when government employment accounts for about one-third of the share of the increase in the female labour force. The increase in government came about largely because of the expansion of the elementary and secondary educational activities of government. The post-war baby-boom children, born in 1947, were entering school in the mid- and late 1950s and a vastly increasing educational labour force was needed to staff these schools. Since the 1880s, women have been involved in elevating and civilizing society. When the educational programme expanded to accommodate the children of the baby boom, women played a dominant role in the burgeoning of the welfare-state economy.

(2) The next major period of expansion was the late 1960s. Between 1960 and 1970, the level of government employment of women increased by an additional 5 per cent, from 15 to 20 per cent of the total female labour force. The growth in the governmental sector was again fuelled by a demand for social services. While education continued to be important, other social services came to play an increasingly larger role in the employment of women.

If we look at the period as a whole and focus on race and gender, the changes in the level of employment between 1940 and 1970 are even more dramatic. According to the figures reported in the Decennial Census in 1940, 5 per cent of black women and 12.9 per cent of white women were employed by government. By 1970, 18.7 per cent of all white females were employed by government, and 24.2 per cent of all black females. Public employment between 1960 and 1970 accounted for about half of the net aggregate non-agricultural employment increase for black women as compared with about one-third for white women.

In 1964, the Economic Opportunity Act was passed as American social policy launched its war against poverty. Although the reduction of poverty through a programme of manpower training and community action was the explicit aim of the Economic Opportunity Act, the programme also had employment effects. Critics of the programme interpreted these employment effects as distortions of the legislative intent, but viewed from the perspective of women's ability to enter the labour force, a more positive interpretation is required. It was the War on Poverty that initiated not only a new range of services for the poor, but also expanded the demand for female labour, and especially for black female labour.

(3) The third period, between 1970 and 1980, showed a departure from the steady increase in the direct role of government as an employer of women which had characterized the experience of the previous decades. Government employment for women fluctuated during the 1970s, reaching a high of 23 per cent in 1975. This increase was related to the deep economic recession that occurred around 1974 and 1975. However, after 1975 there was a decline in each year until 1980, when the level of employment rose again. The result of these movements was that by the end of the decade employment was at the same level that it had reached in the beginning of the decade.

No government hires employees without reference to the social group that they represent and the political and social pressure which the group can muster in the system. The way in which 'the Irish took over City Hall' in Boston and the way in which it came about in New York City that the sanitation department was dominated by Italians, the police force by the Irish, and the schools by the Jews is part of our national folklore. We might reasonably expect, therefore, to find pressure from an active Women's movement for the employment of women. The affirmative-action machinery of the Sixties provided a ready vehicle for such pressure.

Freeman observes, 'No institutional change has transformed the labor market more than the outlawing of discriminatory employment practice by Title Seven of the Civil Rights Act of 1964 and the requirement that federal contractors engage in affirmative action under Executive Order 11246'.[15] We might imagine that government itself would be especially responsive in this climate of regulation.

However, there is no direct empirical evidence to show that it was the affirmative-action programme for women of the 1960s that made the amount of government employment of women much larger than that of the private economy.

Women are 42 per cent of all persons employed in civilian non-agricultural jobs. They are over-represented in government where they total 48 per cent of all government employees (52 per cent at state and local-government levels, but only 33 per cent at the federal level), but under-represented in the private sector where they make up 37 per cent of the employed. It is not only that women are more likely to work for government, but also that most of the good jobs that women hold are in this sector with government employing half of all the professional women in the United States. It is also true, however, that poor-paying jobs are concentrated in the public sector. On this question, an Equal Employment Opportunity Commission (EEOC) report observes that 'equal employment opportunity has not yet been fulfilled in state and local government. The 1975 data reveal that minorities and women continue to be concentrated in relatively low paying jobs, and even when employed in similar positions, they generally earn lower salaries than whites and men respectively.'[16]

But this argument may be too simplistic. Lester Thurow attempts to calculate the level of government wages that would be paid if every occupational skill in government were paid exactly what the same level of skill can earn in the private economy; and reaches a very different conclusion than that reported by EEOC. Thurow observes that even when one corrects for skills, the federal government pays women 20 per cent more than the private sector does. Minority females end up with an even larger premium — around 30 per cent in the federal government. The situation, however, is different at the state and local-government levels. The premium for white females in local government disappears and only a small premium of 5 per cent is retained for non-white women. He concludes that government or more specifically the federal government raises the earnings of women and minorities above what they would be if only the private sector were to exist.[17]

Even though government is not hiring women in the same spirit that the city of Boston once hired Irishmen, nevertheless government and especially local government is hiring women. As we have pointed out, local government is employing women 'to man' (if one can use that term in this context) the expanding social-service activities.

Women in the public sector work primarily in social services. But if social-service activities are important in the employment of women, then to focus only on direct government employment is misleading, since government finances similar programmes in the profit and non-profit sectors. In order to discuss this phenomenon, we propose a new analytic concept — the idea of a *social welfare economy*. In the American context, social-welfare activities take place at three different sectors: (a) government, especially at the state and local levels; (b) the non-profit sector where government contracts to run institutions to render services which were largely financed by government but administered by non-governmental and non-profit bodies; and (c) a private, proprietary sector which is explicitly concerned with rendering a service for profit. The boundaries separating these sectors are fuzzy, because government indirectly contributes to the growth of the other two sectors. We need therefore to distinguish between the welfare state and the social-welfare labour market. The latter is characterized by the provision of services regardless of institutional auspices. Focusing on a service society rather than the service state, we get very different insights about the contribution of services to the increase in the employment of women.

The role of government with respect to women's employment is much broader than government's role as a direct employer, for government is deeply involved in the non-profit sector of the social-welfare labour market.

The government role in the non-profit sector is much broader than the special tax status it offers these institutions. Government is also an important source of revenue for non-profit bodies. Tracing the role of government in creating and sustaining the non-profit sector, outside of the tax arena, is complicated because data has not been assembled to consider this question explicitly. This may change in the future as the weakness of the present accounting schemes becomes clear. But we can piece together parts of the story about government's role. The fragmented evidence shows we need to add direct government grants to the traditional forms of government contracts and purchases as new sources of revenue to the non-profit sector. For example, there has been a marked increase in the grant-in-aid system with 'a massive proliferation in the numbers and types of entities ... special districts, non-profit corporations, etc. that . . . are now eligible for direct grant assistance'.[18] Equally important is the indirect role of the government transfer programmes to consumers who then use these resources to purchase goods and services from the social-welfare segment of the non-profit sector.

A recent study of the non-profit sector in five cities and five functional areas suggests that government revenues account for one-third of the income of the non-profit sector; fees for services, an additional third;[19] and private charity, the remaining third. Government resources are clearly important for non-profit organizations that operate in the social-welfare labour market. This suggests that we should combine government and the non-profit sector as an indirect expression of government initiative.

Between 1940 and 1980, the industry grew from 7 to 18 per cent of the labour force, thus accounting for one-quarter of the nation's net job increase.

In those years the social-welfare industry created jobs for one out of every three women entering the labour force compared with only one out of every seven men.

In 1940, women comprised 59 per cent of the social-welfare labour market's 3 million workers. By 1980, 70 per cent of the nations 17.3 million workers employed in human service industries were women. The social-welfare labour market is strikingly more feminized in the period between 1940 and 1980 than is the general labour force.

The Future of the Social Welfare Labour Market

Government appears to be taking a different budgetary tangent during the 1980s than it has in the past. Three major changes have occurred: defence expenditures have increased, taxes have decreased, and there is anxiety about letting the deficit rise. Given these developments, it seems almost inevitable that the size and rate of growth of the social-welfare labour market will decline, and these trends will affect the economic position of women.

Two contradictory patterns can be identified, depending on whether we focus upon the changing provider/employer mix or the changing capacity of the economy to generate jobs. Selective budgetary cuts for means-tested social-welfare programmes will create a situation where fewer women and fewer poor women are recipients of social services. What effect will the changing pool of recipients have on women as functionaries of the social-welfare labour market? One possible interpretation is that the social-welfare labour market will become even more privatized and more feminized in the future than it has in the past. But, if such a pattern develops, it seems reasonable to speculate that the social-welfare labour market will also provide fewer jobs for poor women and for black women. According to this scenario there is a direct and mutually reinforcing role between the state as provider and the direct and indirect role of the state as employer. This implies that the social-welfare labour market will both hire fewer black women and provide fewer benefits for them, and it will also provide fewer resources for poor women whether they are black or white, and hire fewer poor women as workers. Thus the blacks as functionaries, and the poor blacks and whites as recipients, will be the losers when government tries to trim the size of the social-welfare labour market.

On the other hand, if the economy's capacity to generate jobs decreases, and if government in the future, as it has in the past, shows a willingness to provide jobs for men by expanding the social-welfare labour market, then the social-welfare labour market may become both less privatized and less feminized.

Conclusion

We have argued that women are today involved in the State and the State is involved in society in such a way that the relationship between women and the State is complex. The interests of women are not unitary. The State is not a single body acting in unison; it institutionally includes: courts, legislatures, administrative and regulatory agencies; and social-service institutions created by the direct and indirect role of the State. None of these singly, and much less the State as a whole, is likely to have a coherent policy about virtually anything; it certainly has none on women. Whether we think of the State as a single body reconciling conflicting interests, or as itself constituted by a cluster of institutional actors with specialized interests, a 'policy towards women' will not be forthcoming.

The Women's Research and Educational Institute of the Congresswoman's Caucus, in analysing the impact on women of the administration's proposed budget, is asserting a political interest for women across race and class. Their analysis takes the diverse groups of recipients — black AFDC mothers, white Medicaid recipients, and working mothers receiving fuel subsidies, food stamps, and school lunches for their children — as a common group. The Caucus sees them as common recipients and would like to see them mobilized on the basis of gender so as to protect their common interest as women.

Not only are women disporportionately in the recipient role; they are also disproportionately in the provider role. Thus there is a latent politics linking providers and receivers in the social-welfare labour market. Claiming around this issue has the potential for producing a distinctively women's vote.

While the two issues of the provider and employer roles are factually linked, it is not clear that they can be politically linked and serve to mobilize a distinctively women's interest in the role of the State. Off in the wings, are the other issues of concern to women — taxation, job-market regulation (occupational health and safety, the structure of fringe benefits, entry, promotion, pay tenure, hours, etc.), and the laws and regulations around contraception and abortion. The State enters all the domains that are important to women. Some of these issues become politicized. For example, the questions around family planning become redefined as an issue of feminist politics and the very naming of the phenomenon is transformed from family planning to reproductive rights.

The politics of gender has been evolving rapidly and is enormously complex. Women's claims intersect in diverse ways with the actions of the State in all its various roles: as provider, as regulator, and as employer. Some issues, such as legislation on abortion (whichever way this goes), obviously involve the State and have become clearly defined as the concern of women, but such issues do not only concern women and the State. Others, such as taxation and pensions, which have profound implications for women, are not usually thought of as women's issues. Women are divided by class, by age, and by race, so as to produce with respect to the actions of the State differing women's interests rather than a single homogeneous interest group. Finally, women's overt claiming in the political and economic realms has been complicated by the set of conventional understandings as to women's natural roles, abilities, and concerns; claiming has had to involve a renegotiation of the natural.

In the next chapter we examine some of the difficulties experienced, under these conditions, in building a movement which would make women a *collective* force for claiming.

NOTES

[1] Barbara Allen Babcock, Ann E. Freedman, Eleanor Holmes Norton, Susan C. Ross, *Sex Discrimination and the Law: Causes and Remedies*, Boston: Little, Brown and Co., 1975, pp. 9-10.
[2] 'Civil Servants and Contract Employees: Who Should do What for the Federal Government', US General Accounting Office, 19 June 1981, p. 2.
[3] Sheldon Danziger, Robert Haveman, and Robert Plotnick, 'Income

Transfer Programs in the United States: An Analysis of their Structure and Impact', Joint Economic Committee, Congress of the United States Special Study on Economic Change, Volume 6, *Federal Finance: The Pursuit of American Goals*, Washington, DC: US Government Printing Office, 23 December 1980, Table 4, p. 238.

[4] Robert M. Ball, *Social Security Today and Tomorrow*, New York: Columbia University Press, 1978, pp. 311 and 315.

[5] See also Warren Weaver, Jr., 'Women's Benefits: Debate is Rekindled', *New York Times*, 4 June 1981.

[6] *Social Security Bulletin*, Annual Statistical Supplement, 1977-79, Social Security Administration, US Department of Health and Human Resources, September 1980, Table 55, p. 108.

[7] Ibid., p 75.

[8] For a thoughtful analysis, see Gregory Berman, 'Women Cheated by Social Secutiry', *In These Times*, 1-14 July 1981, p. 19.

[9] Phyllis Wallace, *Equal Employment Opportunity and the AT&T Case*, Cambridge, Mass.: MIT Press, 1976.

[10] Linda Greenhouse, 'Court's Sex Rulings: A Subtle Setback', *New York Times*, 1 July 1981.

[11] Danzinger *et al.* op. cit. p. 238.

[12] Jo Freeman, *The Politics of Women's Liberation: A Case Study of an Emerging Social Movement and Its Relation to the Policy Process*, New York: David McKay Company, 1975.

[13] Babcock *et al.*, p. 578.

[14] The primary source of data we review in this chapter comes from an annual survey conducted by the Department of Commerce of establishments. This survey excludes agricultural workers. It is only since 1964 that the established series included information on the employment of women. Prior to these years, the only available information on the employment of women comes from surveys of households from the United States Decennial Census and the annual Current Population Survey (CPS). The different data sources yield remarkably different pictures of the level of government employment of women. In 1977, the CPS question regarding longest job held in the preceding year yields a government labour force of 8,981; the average monthly employment question shows 7,412 government employees and the Establishment survey 6,984 thousand. Thus there is a 30 per cent difference in the level of government employment of women depending on the source of data. If the series on year-round, full-time employment of women is used, the figure declines to almost half the number reported in the longest job series — 4,444. The figures we report are biased on the conservative side, because the size of the governmental sector is smallest in the establishment survey.

[15] Richard B. Freeman, 'The Evolution of the American Labor Market: 1940-80', in Martin Feldstein (editor), *The American Economy in Transition*, Chicago: University of Chicago Press, 1980, p. 376.

[16] *Minorities and Women in State and Local Government, 1975*, Volume One, Statistical Summary, United States Equal Employment Opportunity Commission, Washington, DC: US Government Printing

Office, 1977, p. 111.

[17] Lester C. Thurow, *Zero Sum Society: Distribution and the Possibilities for Economic Change*, New York: Basic Books, Inc., 1980, p. 165.

[18] Lester M. Salamon, 'Rethinking Public Management: Third Party Government and the Changing Forms of Government Action', *Public Policy*, Summer 1981, p. 3.

[19] Julian Wolpert and Thomas A. Reiner, 'The Metropolitan Philadelphia Study, Final Report', Table 27, p. 54. Regional Science Department: University of Pennsylvania, July 1980.

CHAPTER 6

The Women's Movement as a Process of Claiming

IT would be attractive to imagine the process of claiming as one in which a number of persons in a society become aware of a shared deprivation or simply decide to press for a larger share and organize together to forward their demands. The imagery is Chartism: here come the marchers, with their banners and petitions. On second thoughts, we realize that the means of claiming may be much more diverse; women have hired lobbyists, signed petitions, placed advertisements, marched, disrupted the stock market — all ways of claiming. But in this social-movement view of claiming, the points to be understood are the traditional organizing issues: how do a certain category of persons come to sense a common interest and to constitute an organized group capable of exerting pressure? And what means do they employ, once organized, to forward their ends? And what consequences does successful claiming have on the movement and on the interest groups attached to it?

But the process of claiming turns out to be more intricate than even this modified picture would suggest. A social movement may have as part of its history its particular banners, petitions, and demonstrations, but it is also and necessarily interwoven with the changing rules, institutions, and ideas in the rest of society. Any claiming process takes place within an existing claims system, itself far from static, which affects the movement in the content of its claims, the style and strategy of its claiming, and the composition of its membership.

The existing claims system does this in a number of ways. It regulates the process of claiming, both through rules and procedures of legitimate claims-making, and by way of the characteristics of the institutions through which claiming takes place. The existing structure of claims brings with it explicit or potential interest groups with reference to what is; these interest groups compete and collaborate in various ways with new groups of claimants or extended claims by older groups. The existing system of claims furthermore structures the terms of argument as to the legitimate, the controversial, and the inconceivable.

This variety of potential interests and the various institutional channels and rationales of claiming form for any individual a set of possibilities, rather than a clear-cut set of objectives and allegiances. Women, for example, are not a homogeneous group but divided by class, race, and other characteristics, and in a world where men hold the major resources it has always been deeply problematic whether the interests of any particular woman lie with a primary identification to other women. 'Sisterhood is powerful' is a movement slogan, not a factual assertion. There has always been not one but several women's movements, and a majority of women would consider themselves part of none (when the slick feminist magazine *Ms.* surveyed its readers in 1972 and 1973, 83 per cent of the first respondents and 76.6 per cent of the second said they were not members of a movement group).[1]

'Once a social movement enters the political realm', so Freeman tells us, 'it is usually constrained by the limitations of that realm. There already exist many concrete, accepted "rules of the game" which newcomers are expected to abide by.'[2] The rules can be changed; she points out that political pamphleteering, illegal in the seventeenth and eighteenth centuries, became legalized, that the strike and boycott, once seditious, have come to be protected. But at any given time, the existing institutional rules constrain and shape action.

Furthermore — and this is particularly salient for the women's movement — behind the explicit institutional rules there are the customs, cultural categories, and socially transmitted systems of motives which constitute the realm of the natural. It is possible to describe this realm and its social relationships as a system of claims rationales and established claim entitlements, but claiming in this realm appears as inter-personal and intra-psychic rather than as a political activity. It takes a good deal of consciousness-raising to see 'You don't care . . .' as part of a claiming movement.

The existing realm includes not only rules and procedures which are accepted (and the categorization of alternatives as out of order), but also established and legitimized bodies which constitute the framework for action. For example, it made a difference to women's claiming that the *Equal Pay Act of 1963* was administered through the existing machinery of the Wage and Hour Division of the Employment Standards Administration of the Department of Labor, providing for anonymity to complainants, rapid handling of complaints, and periodic routine reviews of employers, whereas Title VII of the *Civil Rights Act*, prohibiting discrimination in employment, was administered by the new Equal Employment Opportunity Commission, which required, for active enforcement on behalf of women, substantial organized pressure from outside the agency[3] — a 'social gap' eventually filled by the National Organization for Women (NOW).

Thus, the character of the existing claims system and of the social institutions which constitute it shapes the way in which new claims come to be made, are in their turn institutionalized, or are deflected or repressed.

It may often occur that one group of persons make a claim on behalf of another group, either because the first set derive some advantage from being the representatives of the second, or because the principle involved is one of general extension, and therefore important to keep open for the claimant group. The American Civil Liberties Union has sponsored over three hundred sex-discrimination cases;[4] its basic interest is not in the status of women, but in the maintenance and extension of civil liberties on an equal basis.

Claims for one group of persons may get established as a secondary consequence of establishing the claims of others. 'The Equal Pay Act came about more out of a concern for men than for women. Although first proposed in 1869, at the National Labor Union Convention, equal pay did not become an issue until World War I . . . Since women traditionally worked for less money than men, the 2 million to 4 million women suddenly added to the work force created a concern that they would depress wage rates and that men would be forced to work at the lower rates after the war.'[5] The same argument surfaced at the time of World War II. It has, indeed, been argued that the major effect of the bill was to increase the job security of men by discouraging employers from replacing men by lower-paid women.

Claiming groups use political and legal pressure to bring about the institutionalization of rights, but the process may also run in reverse; the claiming group may come into existence to make use of a claims framework which has been established. The National Organization for Women, a major women's advocacy organization, came into existence in 1956 around the legal basis for contesting sex-segregated want ads provided by Title VII of the *Civil Rights Act* and its enforcement arm, the Equal Employment Opportunity Commission. On 18 August 1965, the EEOC issued guidelines forbidding newspapers to carry separate racial headings for want ads. A memorandum from the Citizens' Advisory Council on the status of women, supported by the Interdepartmental Committee on the Status of Women, urged that this principle be extended to classification by sex. The EEOC refused, arguing that 'these column headings do not prevent persons of either sex from scanning the area of the "jobs available" page'. NOW was incorporated largely around the issue and immediately organized a campaign around sex-segregated want ads, involving lobbying, picketing, public hearings, demonstrations, and legal action. By the time (9 August 1968) the EEOC had been forced to issue new guide-lines, NOW had grown substantially in membership and broadened its concerns to a wider range of women's issues.[6]

Successful claiming creates its own momentum, in part because the channels of claiming become strengthened, and in part because their existence supports the active mobilization of constituencies which can press for enforcement. 'The acceptance of sex discrimination as a legitimate area of concern rather than as a competitor for scarce resources with race discrimination' by the Equal Employment Commission 'was in part due to the changing climate of opinion stimulated by the women's liberation movement, in part to the hiring of many young attorneys, especially women, who were open to new ideas, and in part to the impact of the cases themselves'.[7]

It has been noted that the Equal Employment Opportunity Commission took as its original mandate issues of race discrimination and only slowly, and with very considerable prodding, took on issues of discrimination by sex. Within less than a decade the EEOC issued a massive report on discrimination by the American Telegraph and Telephone Company which, according to the head of the task force responsible for the report, advanced a

> ... really revolutionary view of sex discrimination. We took more or less hook, line and sinker the feminist view as espoused by the National Organization for Women — their view of institutionalized sex discrimination — and we said we wanted to attack it at its roots in the Bell System. Not just equal pay for equal work, etc. We wanted to present the whole sociology and psychology of sexual stereotypes as it was inculcated into the Bell System structure.[8]

The task-force members had originally been educated to this 'revolutionary view' by feminist lawyers within the EEOC. Once convinced of its value they had held meetings with NOW leaders arranged by Catherine East of the CACSW. The impact of these meetings is evident not so much in the final financial settlement (which NOW denounced) as in the final insistence that future Bell System employment practices integrate men into women's jobs as well as advance women into men's. Previously, the orientation of the EEOC had been solely to advancing minorities and women into better jobs, while ignoring those poorly paid jobs held primarily by minorities and women. It was NOW that convinced them that any job category that remained solely female (or black) would contribute to the maintenance of sex-role and race stereotypes and with that the psychological aspects of discrimination.[9]

Thus claims tend to expand, because claiming groups become organized around the claims process, and because the rationales of claim categories become developed in the process of claims-making.

But at the same time, the claiming process also sets off backlash and counter-claims. Organized pressure for affirmative action on behalf of women by universities and colleges began to build in early 1970. Over two years, the HEW Office of Contract Compliance expanded from roughly twenty to sixty people nationally and a special Higher Education Division was set up in it in the summer of 1972.[10] But in May of 1972, representatives of six Jewish organizations met with the Secretary of HEW to voice their concern about 'abuses' of affirmative-action guide-lines. 'That summer they filed over their complaints with HEW charging white males were denied jobs or promotions due to preferential treatment for women and minorities by colleges trying to meet the affirmative action regulations.'[11] The Bakke case was a notable example of claims limitation through the courts.

The fact that at any time the given institutional and legal channels of claiming are finite, means that the relationships between groups making similar claims are inherently both collaborative and competitive. They are collaborative in that the establishment of claims rationales and enforcing institutions for one becomes the basis for claiming by the other. They are competitive in that each group will plausibly wish to maximize its own particular share of such resources as platform time, movement resources, and affirmative action jobs.

The claims of women and the claims of Blacks have been linked in American political history by sharing a set of claiming institutions. One of the more consequential examples of this linkage is also one of the most absurd: the addition of 'sex' to the prohibited categories of discrimination in the *Civil Rights Act of 1964* was the work of a conservative southern Congressman who hoped to defeat the bill by making it unacceptable to many liberals. When the bill, contrary to prediction, went on to pass, women and racial minorities together had a new vehicle for claiming.

Successful claiming for one group, Blacks, also creates conditions for further claims both in intellectual structure — claims rationale and doctrines of right — and in organized social support for the other. In October 1967, after relatively modest efforts by women's advocate groups, President Johnson amended the compliance activities of contracting agencies of the federal government to include sex discrimination. 'According to some sources this relatively easy success was largely due to the precedent of Title VII. Since sex was now added to race, religion and national origin in one piece of major legislation, its addition to others was facilitated.'[12]

But the linkage between the claims of women and of racial minorities has also been one of competition. Abolitionism in the nineteenth century and the civil-rights movement in the twentieth were both claiming movements centred on Blacks which came to constitute a kind of 'entering wedge' for the claims of women to social and political equality; in both, women found their particular claims squeezed out by a focus on the claims of minorities. In the course of both movements, women were radicalized as feminists by finding that their support of the claims of Blacks did not entitle them to an equal support for their own claims from those active in the movement for social change. At the 1840 World Anti-Slavery Convention in London, women delegates, including Lucretia Mott and Elizabeth Cady Stanton, were relegated to the galleries and were not permitted to speak. 'As Lucretia Mott and Elizabeth Cady Stanton wended their way arm in arm down Great Queen Street that night . . . they agreed to hold a women's rights convention on their return to America.'[13] The result was the Seneca Falls Women's Rights Convention of 1848, which opened the women's suffrage movement and articulated a broad spectrum of women's claims in the language of the Declaration of Independence. A similar sequence of events characterized the movements of the 1960s. Women working in the civil-rights struggles in the South sometimes resented the 'tendency to assume that housework around the freedom house would be performed by women'[14] and that in the sexual mores of the period 'the boundary between sexual freedom and exploitation was a thin one'.[15] The experience of Mott and Stanton was repeated as women within SDS began to resent and protest the lack of equality between men and women in the Left. At an anti-war rally in 1969, a woman speaker was not kept in the gallery (like Mott and Stanton in 1840), but when she tried to speak men shouted, 'Take her off the stage and fuck her.'[16] In the nineteenth century women who campaigned to get the word 'sex' added to the proposed amendment which would prohibit the denial of suffrage on account of race had been discouraged from doing so in the words: 'This is the Negro's hour.' In the same way, in the 1967 National Conference for a New Politics the resolution committee refused to introduce the women's statement, but went on to give the floor to a speaker on American Indians. 'Then William Pepper patted Shulie (Shulasmith Firestone) on the head and said "Move on little girl; we have more

important issues to talk about here than women's liberation."
... We had a meeting the next week with women in Chicago.'[17] Thus the dominance of racial minorities' interests in both these claiming movements drove women away from collaborative efforts, and towards an independent women's movement.

The history of the women's movement shows clearly that one of the basic elements in the claiming process is an intellectual one: a definitional element, involving the development of claims categories and the establishment of these new categories as legitimate parts of the domain of political argument. In part, the women's movement has consisted of claiming for women rights analogous to those to which men have already made claim – the vote, admission to institutes of higher learning, equal pay for equal work. In part it has consisted in establishing as legitimate topics of politics, as areas for claiming, issues which had previously been treated socially as 'personal' or 'natural' and thus beyond the reach of politics. Because of the importance of the legitimacy or illegitimacy of claims categories, the women's movement as a process of claiming has always had a double character; we may, like Hole and Levine, counterpose the movement for 'women's rights' to the movement for 'women's liberation'.

The women's movement appears in its 'women's rights' aspects as a political constituency, pressing for specific alterations in the structure of power and resource distribution: appointment of women to high office, affirmative action in jobs, equal pay for equal work.

Then, women's claiming attaches to already defined social categories of entitlement, and asks for women rights which others have already acquired or are demanding.

But feminism also raises new issues and new claiming categories. The involvement of women with domestic and interpersonal work leads feminists to create turbulence in all sorts of existing social arrangements to a degree not nearly as characteristic of other claiming movements. For example: a review of women's opportunities in the legal profession[18] presents as a serious barrier the practice in law offices of expecting substantial overtime work. 'If a parent does not want to relinquish substantial opportunity to care for and be with her children, or if she cannot free herself from child care responsibilities, a limited weekly commitment to the labor market is essential. However, in law practice limiting the hours one is available for work adversely affects one's ability to be promoted or to obtain significant and stimulating assignments.'[19] It thus appears that a claim to job equality for women in the legal profession suggests a restructuring of the apportionment of commitments between family and work among lawyers in general.

The National Organization for Women, an organization which began around employment-related issues moved, although certainly not without bitter internal struggles, into reproductive issues which some of its founders had seen as inappropriate for an 'NAACP type organization'.[20] The 1967 NOW conference supported abortion-law repeal. In 1971, NOW passed a resolution declaring that 'a woman's right to her own person includes the right to define and express her own sexuality and to choose her own life-style; therefore we acknowledge the oppression of lesbians as a legitimate concern of feminism'.[21]

In this case, as in others, claiming creates its own momentum. A movement comes into existence, and as it experiences some successful claiming its adherents experience a sense of efficacy which encourages them to bring new issues forward for claiming. But if the issues are sufficiently novel, they do not fit within the existing institutional channels of claiming and the existing claims rationales.

The 'women's meetings' of the sixties provided a setting in which the categories of personal politics could develop.

In sharp contrast to the new left ideological debates from which they had been excluded, women found, for the first time, that they could legitimately talk about themselves, their relationships, their hopes and angers. One participant, pointing out the difference between women's liberation and other movements, noted that women 'are thrilled, literally by the certain knowledge that for once, this is their battle in which they can organize and fight without the constant struggle of being an outsider playing a dual role'.[22]

For the women involved in these meetings, the freedom from established categories was both exhilarating and alarming.

This was a movement without barriers. The young women had not

The Women's Movment as a Process of Claiming 111

begun with a legalistic definition of 'women's rights'. They were radicals, used to taking on issues and getting down to their roots whatever the cost. And they began with a high level of shared cultural alienation . . . . 'Freedom' and 'liberation' were absolutes — to be fought for and won. But whom would they fight? Men? Their husbands and boyfriends? The rest of the left? The consumer society? Maybe even themselves as well. While some women claimed their new strength joyfully, others cringed inwardly, wanting independence but insecure about their capacity to sustain it, fearful that no one could love an independent woman, afraid to test their conviction against male ridicule and rage.[23]

Betty Friedan's *The Feminine Mystique*, on the malaise of the suburban housewife, came out in 1963. In a preface to the tenth-anniversary edition of the book, she wrote:

Until I started writing the book, I wasn't even conscious of the women problem. Locked as we all were then in that mystique, which kept us passive and apart, and kept us from seeing our real problems and possibilities, I, like other women, thought there was something wrong with *me* because I didn't have an orgasm waxing the kitchen floor . . . After I finished the second chapter, a part of me would wonder, Am I crazy . . .[24]

The development of a new political language for women's claims changed politics, made political and problematic what had been seen as natural, and altered the situation of women by making it possible for them to think what had been unthinkable.

'Personal politics' challenges the prevailing definitions of the political. Lenin complained to Clara Zetkin, leader of the German women's socialist movement, about deficiencies in the 'proletarian class-consciousness' of German socialist women. He had heard with dismay of an attempt to organize prostitutes; 'Are there really no industrial working women left in Germany who need organizing?' Still worse, Lenin went on, 'I have been told that at the meetings arranged for reading and discussing with working women, sex and marriage problems come first. They are said to be the main objects of interest in your political instruction and educational work. I could not believe my ears when I heard that.'[25] The struggle to establish such 'personal' issues as the abortion law, gynaecological practice, and the division of labour within the family as the subject of politics has had to compete with prevailing definitions of the proper realm of politics. Commenting on the women's movement of the Progressive Era, Firestone says: 'By seeing the W.R.M. as only tangent to another, more important politics, they were in a sense viewing themselves as defective men: women's issues seemed to them "special", "sectarian", while issues that concerned men were "human", "universal".'[26]

If 'personal politics' challenges the established definition of the political, it equally challenges the established boundary of the natural.

Sex class is so deep as to be invisible. Or it may appear as a superficial inequality, one that can be solved by merely a few reforms, or perhaps by the full integration of women into the labor force. But the reaction of the common man, woman and child — *That?* Why you can't change *that!* You must be out of your mind — is the closest to the truth.... This gut reaction — the assumption that, even when they don't know it, feminists are talking about changing a fundamental biological condition — is an honest one.[27]

In *The Politics of Women's Liberation*, Jo Freeman says that 'a successful movement provides an *intersection* between personal and social change'.[23] But a social movement is not wholly free to reorganize personal consciousness by bringing personal issues into the framework of politics any more than it is wholly free to restructure society; in both the personal and the societal realms any movement operates from the limitations and potentialities of what is. A movement which tries to change the consciousness of women, to build self-confidence, a sense of autonomy and assertion, must do so in a world in which female occupations pay less than men's, in which men hold the majority of positions of power in society, and in which women are deeply involved in nurturing children and, somewhat less overtly, 'their' men, and derive real rewards from that effort. At the same time, the women's movement, and changes in women's consciousness at the personal level, are consequence as well as cause: the outcome of economic changes which have propelled women into the paid labour market, and made the family less and less the controller of resources which could provide long-term security to anyone, including women. The capacity to claim in new ways must rest, at some implicit level, on changes in the structure of realizable interests.

Women's 'special place' in the claiming realm of the family makes for a complicated and problematic interaction between movements for women's rights and for women's liberation at the societal level, and between self-images of femininity and feminism within women as individuals. Women's commitment to 'domestic responsibilities' within the family weakens women's attachment to work and career-building, supporting gender discrimination in the occupational structure and in earnings. If women's jobs pay less than men's and carry less status and power with them, this fact alone reduces women's bargaining power within the family, and encourages women to make the best of what might be a bad bargain. In the world of work and politics, women claim in the language of equality and universalism; within the family, women claim in the language of personalism and need for protection. Women's attitude towards the family will therefore vary with their position in the world of work; and women's attitude towards work will vary with the degree of power and security provided by the family.

The interaction between the economic and political and the familial and personal extends into issues at the most personal level, creating a complex politics of reproductive rights and claims.

Feminists always have to balance the gains and losses from struggles for contraception and abortion against the other problems women face such as unequal employment opportunity, unequal wealth, unequal education, and unequal domestic responsibilities. Thus, a position appropriate to one historical era is not appropriate in another when the balance of women's needs and possiblities has changed.[29]

From the modern perspective, it is strange to realize that in the last two decades of the nineteenth century, women were important in the criminalizing of abortion and in restricting the dissemination of contraceptives. Women were active on behalf of the movements for 'social purity', striving to improve the moral level of both the home and society by raising the age of consent for girls, campaigning against liquor and prostitution, and demanding a restricted sexuality within marriage.[30] That women should take the lead in opposing contraception has been interpreted[31] as representing women's need to maintain the link between sexuality and reproduction in a day when marriage was the primary basis of women's livelihood. An alternative interpretation has the woman opposing contraception for reasons 'primarily ideological and moral'.[32] In either interpretation, the women-led movements against contraception and for 'social purity' must be understood in the context of a world in which women had few alternatives outside marriage. 'For women's "control over their own bodies" to lead to a rejection of motherhood as the *primary* vocation and measure of social worth required the existence of alternative vocations and sources of worthiness.'[33] 'Women's activity on behalf of Social Purity was . . . quite in conformity with the doctrine of separate spheres, as other causes like woman sufferage, would never be. For voting was not a part of domestic morality — that was man's sphere.'[34] It is not unreasonable, therefore, to find that many women opposed woman suffrage.[35] The nineteenth-century feminists who promoted 'social purity' and the 'civilizing mission of womanhood' both within the family and without saw women's claims domain as squarely within the family. Only gradually did feminist movements come into existence which brought forward women's claims to rights arising outside the family sphere.

The feminism of the 1870s had sought to remake marriage in the image of its traditional claims: permanent and monogamous, with dignity and power for women within it, retaining the separate functions of the sexes, and instituting a single standard. In one sense the voluntary motherhood advocates were reactionary because they associated the empowerment of women with the restoration of a preindustrial family-centered society. But at the same time they were driving wedges into the old patriarchial unity of the couple. Decrying rape within marriage, insisting on women's right to refuse, often recommending separate beds and even bedrooms, they were not sentimentalizing marital togetherness or the couple as an inseparable unit . . . Furthermore they were actively building women's organizations and a women's community and sisterhood . . . The feminist birth controllers of the second decade, by contrast, actually looked forward to a weakening of the traditional family through the increasing socialization of work outside the home. They too insisted upon a single standard but they sought it in the removal of repression, not in its equal distribution. They welcomed industrial society, with its class, generational and sex conflicts. They experimented with alternatives to marriage and the family...[36]

The anti-abortion and 'pro-family' groups of the 1980s, very largely female in composition, show that the conflicts of the nineteenth century are still with us. The very successes of the women's movement in the sixties helped to generate a new 'lifestyle feminism' among women of the middle class moving into professional jobs.

Many ... middle class women simply by-passed political organizations like NOW and went straight for assertiveness training courses, 'success seminars' and the like which hammered away at the distinctly unfeminist message that 'you have no one to blame but yourself'.
The co-opted individualistic version of feminism helped ensure that the women's movement would remain within the class and generation of women who inherited it.[37]

There is another way in which partial success has the potential to weaken the force of the women's movement. It has been pointed out that there have been within the women's movement two broad general streams: a women's rights stream, locating its claims within the general framework of that which is socially defined as political and economic, and a women's liberation strain, struggling with the re-definition of the natural. In the 1960s the two appeared as quite distinct, but as drawing energy from each other. During the 1970s, there seems to have been some tendency for the two streams to move closer together. 'Feminist groups have retained different styles with the most moderate, institutional groups found as advocates for female rights within other organizations.'[38] But as long as part of women's claims lie within the realm of the natural, outside of what is socially constituted as politics, there is an inherent difficulty for the movement in that success which consists of establishing women's interests within the terms of reference of the formal political institutions. Thus it is reported that a member of the Democratic Women's Caucus dismissed the ideas of one women's movement leader by saying that the latter '"was not even a registered Democrat and had little knowledge of Democratic party politics. Gains in the Democratic Women's Division and party committees would seem insignificant to her." Similarly, nonactivists thought Caucus leaders were "acting like politicians".'[39] 'Success' in establishing claims within the existing claims framework may render it more difficult for a movement to extend the categories and the institutions of claiming.

Meanwhile, in a world in which women earn, on the average, only 59 per cent of what men do on an hour-to-hour basis, the appeal of emancipation to many women may be understandably limited. Most women are still 'only one man away from welfare'. Feminism has still not resolved the interaction between gender and class, and between the claims systems of the family and the realms of work and politics.

The claims of competing groups is not the only mechanism by which claims are limited. There may be competition between kinds of claims as much as between groups. In the case of women, for example, the Equal Rights Amendment's claim to universalism competed with a body of legislation extending special protective values to women which was supported by the ALF-CIO, and by a number of women, both within and outside the organized labour movement. The claims of feminists to 'reproductive rights' have been contested by women supporters of 'pro-life' (anti-abortion) and 'pro-family' movements, and these ideas may struggle for supremacy within particular women. Carole Joffe's work on abortion clinics[40] shows the deep ambivalence which underlies this issue. It is not simply the claims of the pregnant women versus those of the unborn child; within women the claims language of individual freedom and self-determination (Get Your Laws Off My Body) compete with the commitments, much more deeply developed in women than in men, to the nurturing of children and the development of family life.

The process of claiming is also a struggle of ideas, a struggle over the extension and application of various principles or claims rationales. For example, James Block has recently argued that a present crisis of the American family 'has proceeded from the consistent extension of voluntarist principles of autonomy, choice and mutuality — universally approved standards in our liberal culture — to the last traditional institution'.[41] It is not that these principles, or claiming rationales, are bad ones but we must concede, he argues, that their extension into spheres where they were not previously applied makes for trouble, by weakening valued institutions which were sustained by competing principles, and by a natural process, weakening the continued application of those competing principles as well. If we extend the principles of autonomy and voluntarism to the husband and wife, making maintenance of the marital bond a matter of choice, and refusing to allow a husband to exercise authority over his wife, why should we be surprised to find children demanding as their right their own autonomy and freedom of choice, and refusing to accept the authority of parents? The extraordinary violence with which women's struggle for the vote was met, particularly in England, was surely powered by more than a simple fear of the practical consequences of women's voting; the reaction suggests a feeling that the very foundations of society would be undercut if women's entry into political life were legitimized. In retrospect, the reaction appears absurd as well as unjust; yet we may allow it a certain factual basis.

The categories of gender run very deep in the structure of society. The fact that the social categories of gender are built on the basis of natural differences of sex and that the social roles of women are structured pervasively around commitments to the personal and interpersonal means that we tend to think of these things as 'natural' and thus outside the reach of politics and policy. As a result, claims which disturb the traditional definitions of women's rights shake the categories which we feel are most natural and most to be taken for granted.

Even the movement for women's rights, asking for women's rights like the vote, equal pay for equal work, understood to be legitimate demands on the part of men, meant in practice disturbance of the 'natural' relations of men and women. That part of the women's movement which we are calling 'women's liberation', attacking directly the settled understandings of women's nature and natural role, creates turbulence in the categories of thought in many related areas, since gender, one of the basic social categories, enters into the conceptualization of many issues. We will here sketch some examples of this general point, without developing any of them very fully.

One effect of feminism has been, as we have seen, redefinition of politics or, to put it another way, a redrawing of the line between the natural and the subject of policy. 'I would ask her to prepare the bath for me. She would pretend to demur but she would do it just the same.' By beginning a book on *Sexual Politics* with this quotation from a novel by Henry Miller,[42] and defining politics as 'power-structured relationships: arrangements whereby one group of persons is controlled by another',[43] Kate Millett redefined politics. Feminism has brought control of the human body, sexual choice, even positions in intercourse into politics. One result of feminism in the intellectual field has been a series of studies of the political economy of the family and of personal life. It has become possible to discuss 'the politics of domesticity' and 'reproductive politics'.[44] The 'personal politics' of feminism has contributed to an extension of political analysis into many areas which more traditional conceptualization would have ignored. If there is a politics of husbands and wives, surely there is a politics of landlords and tenants, a politics of doctors and patients, a politics of teachers and students, a politics of social workers and clients.

In the field of economics, feminism has contributed to the critical reinterpretation of the concept of work. It is argued that by defining housework as an aspect of social role, as womanliness, we have made it invisible as work, not serious, not valuable. A growing body of literature, arising out of the women's movement, demands that we take housework seriously.

But in trying to take housework seriously, we struggle with the categories of economic measurement. The women's movement, linked as it is to the revival of Marxism in the United States, finds itself in particular difficulties with the Marxist distinction between 'productive' and 'non-productive' work, which threatens to devalue not only housework (except, perhaps, child-bearing and rearing) but also the commercialized services which are the housewife's alternative. Other consequences follow: thus when Hugh Stretton follows the Australian economist Patricia Apps in reinterpreting housework as economically valuable production, a consequence is the heightened importance of housing as productive capital in the framework of planning.[45]

Development economics which comes out of a feminist perspective is calling attention to the importance of women's productive activities in the non-monetized ('subsistence') sector of rural agriculture, and as unpaid workers in the cash-cropping activities of rural families in the developing countries.[46] In so doing, they invite us to reconsider the economic accounting which skews the calculation of 'economic progress' by measuring the increase in production for the market, and neglects the effects of this expansion of market production on producers and consumers (often women) in the subsistence sector. This kind of turbulence has reached the level of institutional adjustments: the World Bank now demands appraisal of the effects of its projects on women. One may imagine that these efforts will tend to support more far-reaching demands for intellectual reordering, as, for example, the position that since measures of economic growth register the monetization of the economy as much as they do production of goods and services, we should develop more qualitative, and more critical, appraisal of what we have called 'progress'.

Mainstream economists have managed rather comfortably with explaining rewards to labour via concepts of marginal productivity and human capital. The women's movement creates turbulence here also. It calls attention to the political and institutional aspects of wage-setting, and directs attention to the occupational division of labour as a societal process which can be argued about, and with respect to which claims can be made. 'Wages' and 'jobs' become conceptually problematic.

Feminism may also create some turbulence in the category of 'art', and, specifically, the boundary between 'art' and 'craft'.

The art historian Douglas Fraser is quoted as distinguishing art and crafts as follows: 'objects of paramount importance' usually associated with 'high spiritual values' can be regarded as art; utilitarian objects produced by 'slow repetitive' processes are classified as crafts. In the main, art is created by men, crafts by women.[47]

It has been noted, in thinking about housework, that one would rarely think of food preparation and serving as a subject for serious aesthetic criticism; the one philosopher of aesthetics who has tried it obviously thought of his attempt as a radical innovation. Feminists are probably somewhat less likely than the average American to think of cookery as a subject worthy of serious consideration by an intelligent person.

In the working categories of daily life, it is evident that a painting by Josef Albers is art; a patchwork quilt, on the other hand, is craft. But how do we know this? Indeed, the comparison is obviously structured to raise the issues, as the two works represent rather similar aesthetic principles.

Let us think about quilts in the context of this way of distinguishing arts from crafts. We would have to note, first, that the two have at the outset very different relationships to the world of art interpretation. The quilt has its placing in the domestic world of women, the Albers painting in the men's world of galleries and art criticism. If the women who made quilts and the relatives and neighbours who admired them saw in them 'spiritual values', these interpretations also remained within the domestic sphere. When quilts were first collected they were thought of by museums and historians as a craft in the framework of folk technology: an ingenious adaptation to materials shortages in a cold climate, and an expression of the maker's skill in construction. When quilts became 'taken up' as folk art, they were experienced in the context of functionalism in art; it was geometric quilts which were admired, as an instance of the same 'form follows function' doctrine which animates Bauhaus interior design and Nervi's writings on the beauty of bridges. As fashions shifted in the art world, representational and appliqué quilts also came to be admired as an ebullient folk art.

But we have a folk art identified not with its makers, but with its collectors.

The current interest in quilts brings forward some additional themes. It is both aesthetic and feminist. We now have books and a film embodying interviews with quilters; these serve both to bring forward the 'spiritual component' in the intentions of quilt-makers, and the (oddly unnoticed) fact that if there is folk art, there must be folk artists.

Is it so much more tedious to make a quilt than to paint an Albers or Vasarely?

Carol Gilligan, at Harvard, has been reinterpreting morality from a feminist perspective. Her starting-point was the 'stages of moral development' elaborated by Lawrence Kohlberg on the model of Piaget's stages of intellectual development. In this scheme, the highest stage is represented by human rights, principles of general societal applicability: nearer to Kant, nearer to God, as one might say. Gilligan finds that women's moral reasoning takes another path. She tells us that 'women's development can be traced through the evolution of a distinct moral language, the language of selfishness and responsibility, which identifies the moral problem not as one of fairness and rights, but rather as one of obligation and care. The infliction of hurt is considered to be selfish and immoral in its reflection of unconcern, while the exercise of care is regarded as the fulfilment of moral responsibility.' From the women's perspective the morality of rights is not a higher stage than the morality of caring; they are different perspectives. While a masculine perspective, like Kohlberg's, may see women's moral judgements as 'inconclusive', 'the morality of rights and non-interference may appear from a women's perspective as a frightening justification of indifference and unconcern'.[48]

It is not only social and psychological concepts which turn out to reflect the categories of gender, and therefore to be subjects for renegotiation, but the conceptualization of the divine as well. Thus 'across the board, from biblical scholarship and religious history to ethics and theology, our religious heritage is being scrutinized, reinterpreted and in some cases overthrown by a number of writers who, from different points of view, agree that the common enemy is patriarchal religion'.[49] There have been, on the simplest level, changes in the roles of men and women in ritual; women ministers are ordained, and Jewish girls, as well as boys, have a ritual of adolescence. But feminist ideas also enter critically into the world of theology. 'Metaphors carry theological freight. Female imagery, stressing nurture and maternal care, conveys a profoundly different sense of the divine than does the image of a distant male sovereign.'[50] Thus, on the one hand, a group of women struggle to develop an abstractly conceptual and gender-neutral language for the concepts conveyed traditionally by such words as 'God the Father', and, on the other hand, others struggle to establish witchcraft as a contemporary nature religion centring on the worship of the Goddess. The swing from one extreme to the other illustrates how unsettling is the entry of gender into traditional and settled areas of belief and action.

A feminist perspective thus has the potential to press for changes not only in the boundary between the realm of nature and the realm of policy, but also in the categories with which we understand the ongoing stream of human activity. Is the raising of these issues of conceptualization a form of claiming? Not exactly, perhaps; for what is being demanded? But we see these reinterpretations as in the broader sense part of what we are calling the claiming process. The discussion by intellectuals of such issues of conceptualization suggests the continual negotiation of reality through which processes at the individual and interpersonal level link with the macro processes at the general societal level which are more generally seen to be the subject of political economy.

They arise out of the efforts of claiming movements to make sense of the world within which they act: by redefining the world they contribute to the structure of and rationales for future claims.

Claiming by Women: Taking Stock

The measurement of progress in women's claims is complicated by ambivalent political motives. On the one hand, there is a desire not to show that too much has been achieved, lest success undermine political determination. The less than enthusiastic reception of evidence from new time budget studies on the increased domestic role of men with working wives is one example. On the other hand, without some measure of moving forward, the energy needed for political mobilization might falter.

In any case, the picture is certainly mixed.

Women have been making claims in all three realms: in the family, in the world of work, and against the state. In all three realms, they have established new claims.

But in all these realms, change has been limited. In the domestic economy, the primary burden of housework and child care still rests on women. In the world of work, the gap between women's earnings and men's has not closed. In the realm of the state, political activity still has difficulty in accommodating issues which are raised by the special conditions of women's lives, rather than issues where women ask for treatment equal to men — and even for these, there is a way to go.

Both the successes in building a women's movement, and its shortfall in achievement, confirm that, as we have argued, it is necessary to think of a *system* of claims, rather than simply particular claiming issues. We see that changes in the structure of claims in one realm produce new claims in another; for example, as married women, especially as mothers of young children, enter the labour force, there is a demand for a renegotiation of rights and responsibilities within the family. But the structure of claims in one realm also acts as a brake on changes in others. For example, women's claiming in the family is impeded by women's weaker position in the labour market: women who are one man away from welfare, will have strong incentives to adapt themselves to the needs of men. On the other hand, as long as, within the family, women are socially typed as warmhearted, long-suffering creatures, particularly specialized by nature to deal with human relationships; and as long as these capacities, exercised within the family, are seen as ones which any normal woman should be able to perform (and therefore as unskilled work), it is hard to argue about the justice of an occupational structure in which there are a variety of people-serving 'women's jobs' which pay badly. As long as both the world of the family and the world of work institutionalize conventions of 'womanly' role and personality organization, it will be hard for a women's movement to treat the issues arising out of the conventions in a political framework; they will appear as inherent in the nature of things, rather than as regulations or policies calling for redress.

This raises, again, as the context of women's victories and failures, the role of ideas as to the natural. We have argued that it is the particular placement of women's roles and women's interests with respect to social conventions as to the 'natural' which has made it difficult for women to build a movement to claim redress. It has been ideas of the natural which divided the women's movement between a part having to do with 'women's rights' and a 'women's liberation' branch, and which has repeatedly made it possible to declare feminist demands 'out of order' in the arena of political life. Ideas of the natural built into women's own aspirations and images of themselves have reduced women's will to claim 'something different'. So ideas of the natural have constituted a brake on claiming.

But here, again, the relationship runs both ways. As the women in the nineteenth century who entered public life via abolitionism stayed on to fight for suffrage and for a better status for women in the family, so in the twentieth century movement participation changes the participants as well as the institutions and the views of non-participants. In the seventies, the women's rights and women's liberation streams seemed to run together. As women play new roles, what might have seemed bizarre a generation or so ago can come to appear natural. As feminist criticism enters the intellectual life and alters — as we have pointed out — fields as diverse as history, art criticism, economics, and psychology, the natural becomes renegotiated and transformed.

Thus there comes to be a kind of subterranean implicit process of claiming, which takes the form of shifting the ground of overt claims via a restructuring of the natural.

NOTES

[1] Jo Freeman, *The Politics of Women's Liberation: A Case Study of an Emerging Social Movement and its Relation to the Policy Process*, New York: David McKay Company, 1975, p. 36.
[2] Ibid., p. 5.
[3] Ibid., pp. 174-90.
[4] Ibid., p. 181.
[5] Ibid., p. 175.
[6] Judith Hole and Ellen Levine, *The Rebirth of Feminism*, New York: Quadrangle Books, 1971, pp. 40-4.
[7] Freeman, p. 188.
[8] Harvey D. Shapiro, 'Women on the Line, Men at the Switchboard: Equal Employment Opportunity Comes to the Bell System', *New York Times Magazine*, 20 May 1973, p. 27. Quoted in Freeman, p. 89.
[9] Freeman, p. 139.

10. Ibid., p. 190.
11. Ibid., p. 200.
12. Ibid., p. 194.
13. Quoted in Hole and Levine, op. cit., p. 5.
14. Sara Evans, *Personal Politics: The Roots of Women's Liberation in the Civil Rights Movement and the New Left*, New York: Random House, 1980, pp. 76-7.
15. Ibid., p. 81.
16. Ibid., p. 224.
17. Ibid., pp. 198-9.
18. Mary Jo Frug, 'Securing Job Equality for Women: Labor Market Hostility to Working Mothers', *Boston University Law Review*, 59:55, 1919.
19. Ibid., p. 60.
20. Freeman, p. 81.
21. Ibid., p. 99.
22. Evans, p. 204.
23. Ibid., pp. 206-7.
24. Betty Friedan, *The Feminine Mystique*, New York: W. W. Norton, 1974, pp. 5-8.
25. Batya Weinbaum, *The Curious Courtship of Women's Liberation and Socialism*, Boston: South End Press, 1978, pp. 57-9.
26. Shulamith Firestone, *The Dialectic of Sex: The Case for Feminist Revolution*, New York: William Morrow and Co., 1970, p. 21.
27. Ibid., p. 1.
28. Freeman, p. 82.
29. Linda Gordon, 'The Long Struggle for Reproductive Rights', *Radical America*, vol. 15, nos. 1 and 2, 1981, p. 85.
30. Carl N. Degler, *At Odds: Women and the Family in America from the Revolution to the Present*, New York: Oxford University Press, 1980.
31. Linda Gordon, *Woman's Body, Woman's Right: A Social History of Birth Control in America*, New York: Grossman Publishers, 1976.
32. Degler, p. 199.
33. Gordon, 1976, p. 115.
34. Degler, pp. 281-2.
35. Ibid., p. 349.
36. Gordon, 1976, p. 388.
37. Barbara Ehrenreich, 'The Women's Movements: Feminist and Antifeminist', *Radical America*, vol. 15, nos. 1 and 2, 1981, pp. 93-101.
38. Patricia Hanratty, *Social Movements, Interest Groups and Political Change: A Case Study of American Party Politics*, Ph.D. dissertation, MIT, 1979, p. 250.
39. Ibid., p. 185.
40. Carole Joffe, 'What Abortion Counsellors Want from their Clients', *Social Problems*, October 1978 and 'Abortion Work: Strains, Coping Strategies, Policy Implications', *Social Work*, November 1979.
41. James E. Block, 'New Shapes of Family Life', *Dissent*, Summer 1981, pp. 350-7.

[42] Kate Millett, *Sexual Politics*, New York: Ballantine Books, 1969, p. 3.
[43] Ibid., p. 31.
[44] Barbara Leslie Epstein, *The Politics of Domesticity: Women Evangelism and Temperance in Nineteenth-Century America*, Middletown Connecticut: Wesleyan University Press, 1981; William Leach, *True Love and Perfect Union: The Feminist Reform of Sex and Society*, New York: Basic Books, 1980; Eli Zaretsky, *Capitalism, The Family and Personal Life*, New York: Harper and Row, 1976; Carl Degler, *At Odds: Women and the Family in America from the Revolution to the Present*, New York: Oxford University Press, 1980; Linda Gordon, *Woman's Body, Woman's Right: A Social History of Birth Control in America*, New York: Grossman Publishers, 1976.
[45] Hugh Stretton, *Urban Planning in Rich and Poor Countries*, New York: Oxford University Press, 1978, pp. 56-8.
[46] Hanna Papanek, 'Development Planning for Women', *Signs: Journal of Women in Culture and Society*, 3, 1: 14-21 (Autumn 1977); Ester Boserup, *Women's Role in Economic Development*, New York: St. Martin's Press, 1974; Frances Dahlberg (ed.), *Woman the Gatherer*, New Haven and London: Yale University Press, 1981.
[47] Donald Cordry, *Mexican Masks*, Austin: University of Texas Press, 1980.
[48] Carol Gilligan, 'Woman's Place in Man's Life Cycle', *Harvard Educational Review*, no. 4, 1979, pp. 421-5.
[49] Mark Silk, 'Is God a Feminist?', *The New York Times Book Review*, 11 April 1982, p. 11.
[50] Ibid., p. 20.

Epilogue

EVERY structure of claims constitutes a distinctive way of organizing, institutionally and intellectually, the overlap and interaction between claiming in the family, claiming in employment, and claiming against the State. Such claims structures not only differ as between one society and another, but also change over time within a single society. Out of various comments on society and social change, we can identify three models of the interrelationship of the three realms as they affect women in the United States. These models are on the one hand stylized descriptions of the world we had and the world we have. They are on the other hand accounts of the natural order of things, and also of societal norms, for in these models ideas of the natural and of the desirable are joined. In addition, each model presents its own categories of understanding and action, and an account of the interests and purposes which animate action.

The first model is a schematic and value-embedded description of the state of things in the late nineteenth century. The central imagery is the man as provider, deriving the economic resources of the family from the world of work; the wife as caretaker, producing goods and services in the non-monetized household economy. Identity for the wife depends on the mothering and wiving role. Unmarried women — daughters — often work, but they remain within the family domain and contribute their earnings to the household pool. When wives contribute to the income pool they do so within the framing of the family, which restricts their activities to taking in boarders, doing laundry, and the like. Although the economic reality may be multiple earners and shared resources the dominant imagery of male as provider is maintained by (1) the social subordination of wage-earning daughters within the family and (2) the blending of wives' financial contributions with unmonetized domestic labour. The State enters in a residual role when the family fails, as in the case of widows and orphans, or when the economy breaks down, as in severe recessions. The State's role is always defined as self-limiting and self-liquidating, designed to get the 'natural' institutions of the family and the economy to work without need of the State.

This model is historically grounded in the economy of the late nineteenth century, still with a substantial agricultural sector, and with paid employment still predominantly in industrial jobs, rather than in the services which were soon to follow.

The second model is grounded in the unexpected period of sustained economic growth which took place after World War II, and which lasted for almost thirty-five years. In this model wives enter the labour force and bid for equity in earnings and in dignity. Wives move towards a position as co-equals in the family economy, while daughters are off in school preparing themselves for an onslaught on the world of work.

The transition from the first model to the second model calls for the renegotiation of the settled arenas of family and work life. The State enters to mediate in these conflicts. The negotiations between individual women and potential employers become the subject of a body of State regulation — affirmative action, equal-pay legislation — in which the State both allies itself with women's claims, and regulates, bureaucratizes, and thus limits the claiming process. At the same time women's new claims within the family realm are played out in the formal arena of family law, and in the legislative struggles over issues as varied as day care and abortion rights. The boundaries of the natural become loose, and are pushed back; the nature of the natural itself becomes the subject for political debate.

The model is historically grounded in the emergence of a service economy. The State's activities are an important component of the broader service economy.

The third model grows out of the discovery of a new evolving reality. This new reality is one of a slower rate of economic growth, the stubborn combination of high levels of inflation and unemployment, a continuing evolution towards a service economy, and an occupational structure extremely resistant to economic equity for women. Slow growth and occupational rigidity reinforce each other in inhibiting a movement towards gender equality.

In this model, the family is one in which both husband and wife work, but while women's labour-force participation is high, attachment is weak and earnings are relatively low; wives' contribution to household income is modest. The solidarity of the family is neither a vital social ideal, nor the prevailing practice. Divorce is frequent. Many women are heading families, and most children spend some portion of their lives in such a female-headed unit. Given the combination of autonomy and low wages, many women and children become the dependants of the State. At the same time, as increased longevity intersects with the tendency for old people not to be cared for in families, the State also intervenes as the provider for the elderly; the demographics of aging are such as to make this also a group predominantly female. The State becomes a woman's provider, although, because of ambivalence about this role, not a very generous one.

This model is historically grounded in the emergence of a yet-to-be named economy, one characterization of which is the zero-growth economy.

These, then, are three models of the social organization of gender in terms of the intersection of three realms: the family, the economy, and the State. Each model is to a degree grounded in a particular historical situation.

We have tried in this book to develop a way of thinking about such models which we have called a theory of claims. Our theory of claims is located in the family of theories of political economy. We want now to contrast our perspective with the two dominant contrasting perspectives — Marxism and neo-classicism.

We may describe each of these perspectives in terms of the vision of the world which it presents, but at a more basic level each perspective is constituted by a set of conceptual tools for understanding. The vision of the world, and the prescriptions for action which result, are set in motion by the very categories of thought by which understanding is achieved.

The Neo-classical Perspective

In the neo-classical perspective individuals make maximizing choices within a world as given. The present occupational structure represents the outcome of past maximizing choices; so determined, it may be bargained with but not argued against. 'The combined assumptions of maximizing behaviour, market equilibrium, and stable preferences, used relentlessly and unflinchingly, form the heart of the economic approach.'[1] (Market demand, human capital, clearing markets, comparative advantage are central categories of thought.)

The nineteenth-century model which might be described by some as a cultural phenomenon, a traditional family, is clearly understandable in the neo-classical frame in terms of comparative advantage in a market economy. The fact that men get paid more than women must, given the categories of economic thought, be taken as evidence that their labour is more productive than that of women. Since women get paid less in paid employment, their comparative advantage lies in marriage and domestic production. Divorce is very disadvantageous. Gender specialization serves the interest of both men and women. Since individuals are maximizing their utility by making such choices in the market framework, State intervention into the price system (as by regulating women's wages) will only increase inefficiency and in the long run reduce the welfare of everyone.

The world of full employment and the renegotiation of gender can be seen in the neo-classical view, in terms of price changes. The relative prices of men's and women's labour shift; domesticity ceases to hold a comparative advantage; a new set of market equilibria – thought of in a different framework of thought as different institutional arrangements – come into being.

This kind of theory has a little difficulty in dealing with the role of the State in such regulatory activities as affirmative action. This sort of intervention appears as exogenous to the market system – either interfering with 'normal' operations of the market or, in a kind of back-door explanation, brought into being by prior changes in market demand for female labour.

When it comes to the third model, societal trends which the women's movement might interpret as political defeats would be viewed as stabilization of price differentials under conditions of slow economic growth. Economics reluctantly assumes its historic role as the dismal science. The only constructive role for government is to do what it can — largely by getting out of the way — to get markets to function again. Reindustrialization becomes the slogan for the new era. Women have to make the best bargains they can in this new economic reality and a compassionate government will catch in its safety net the casualties, making sure not to make the landing so soft as to destroy the natural vitality of the market.

The Marxist Perspective

The Marxist system also begins with economics, but instead of describing economics in terms of individual choices, it describes a system of power and power struggles based on the relations of production, centring on the creating and distribution of 'surplus value'. The central line of argument deals with men, because it has to do with the relationships between workers ('productive' paid workers) and employers in the evolving economy. Given the historic tendency of women to be somewhat marginal to this worker world, there has been a tendency for women to fall somewhat at the margins in the Marxist view of the politics of class struggle.

There seem to be alternative ways of dealing with this historically marginal role of women. One way, of course, is for women to be brought into the labour force and into the labour movement; the Left has traditionally seen the emancipation of women in terms of incorporation into the world of production. An alternative perspective, developed by some Marxists, is to focus on women's role in social reproduction — the physical reproduction of the labour force, the cultural perpetuation of systems of motivation, and social transmission of a given system of societal organization. Some Marxist feminists have developed this perspective to argue for a view which sees women exploited by men within the social relations of reproduction; the terminology for this description is patriarchy.

The Marxist argument was itself historically conditioned; it developed to give an account of the first, nineteenth-century model of society. It is the social process of production rather than the process of reproduction which is the central organizing element, just as in the nineteenth century the dramatic transition in society was that from agriculture and small commerce to a new industrial and urban world based on manufacturing. The struggle for power in the period centred on the organization of this new productive arrangement.

In giving an account of the evolution of modern industrial society, Marxists have had to confront an explosively expanding service sector, the entry of women into the labour market, and the link between the two. In this new historic situation, social reproduction becomes a much more central element, and with it, a new role for the State. Since women are now at work, the State is gradually forced to assume a more active role in social reproduction, first especially in education, later in medical care. Women also encounter the State in its regulatory role as manager of the conflicts and contradictions involved in the transition to this new form of economy. The welfare-provider role of the State offers another channel within which the State can manage the struggle of capital versus labour by managing the poor. The historic role of the State in acting as agent of the dominant class leads to an interest in keeping the costs of social reproduction as low as possible. The State therefore has an interest in maintaining women's wages in the service sector as low as possible, and in having women continue to perform unpaid labour in the sphere of social reproduction. In this view, the position of women is determined not by discrimination, but by structural oppression.

It becomes possible to think of our second model as a social-reproduction economy, not only because services are a dominant form of employment, but also because the struggles over resources which used to characterize the realm of industrial production now characterize the realm of social reproduction in its varied forms — for example, in the politics of schooling, and in the politics of the defence of the suburbs and the life-style they imply.

It becomes the role of women to package and co-ordinate public and private resources in the sphere of social reproduction. The crystallization of women's reproductive functions becomes the basis for political mobilization. Marxists are at present divided as to whether to follow this argument in seeing social reproduction as the institutional basis for women's claims, or to follow the more traditional view in linking the emancipation of women to participation in the realm of production.

The Claiming Perspective

Both the neo-classical view and the Marxist view embody ways of relating the political and the economic. In the neo-classical view, the driving force is prices; in the Marxist view it is the struggle for power within the system of production. Both systems are elegant so long as they remain within their central organizing principles.

The claims perspective which we have been developing has somewhat less coherence and elegance than either of these in part because it does not start with a central organizing principle so much as with an attempt to describe the varieties of organization and ideology in the world we have. In this description of the world we see politics as much influencing economics as the other way round. Hence, we see a large degree of autonomy, to use the Marxist term, in the distribution of the social surplus; we see distribution as determined neither by 'market mechanisms' nor by the social relations inherent in the system of production. Instead, we see struggle and argument in the political realm of distribution as forcing the world of work to accommodate to political and social realities. While it is undoubtedly true that at the margin there is a limit to claiming, because more cannot be distributed than there is in the pot to share, we do not know what that limit is. What strikes us is the enormous looseness in the link between systems of production and systems of distribution.

The claiming framework also differs from both the neo-classical and Marxist views in the understanding of the interests which motivate struggle. Both the neo-classical and Marxist views take interests as given in reality, in the first framework, by prices, in the second, by position in the structure of production. The claiming framework, rather than focusing on primary interests as the moving parts in the system of thought, focuses on the construction of purposes, which is seen as a social process. Social meaning and justificatory rationales for action which we describe as claims activity shape and reshape the interests which they reflect. Women's interests do not have any social reality unless women come to think of themselves and then to act as a claiming category. Interest and purpose are jointly produced, rather than determinately set by prior interests. The system is much more fluid.

In our view, the natural is socially constructed, continually subject to change, and continuously referred to as the natural after it is changed. This way of looking at things presents a number of problems when it comes to prescription. Everything seems to be up for grabs. In the neo-classical and the Marxist camps there is argument as to appropriate purposes and choices, but because each of these frameworks is anchored into a conception of reality it is always possible to believe that a right choice is to be found. The claiming framework provides no such solid ground.

When we look from a claiming perspective at the nineteenth-century model, we see a social construction of the natural which demarcated three separate claiming spheres with distinctive claiming rationales. The State had a minimal regulatory role *vis-à-vis* the economy characterized by rapid industrial growth. The family appeared as a realm outside both politics and economics. Having constructed the family in this role, and placing women squarely within the family, women appear as the custodians of a special domain of the humane and the natural. Talcott Parsons elevated this to the 'expressive role'.[2]

But this construction of separate and distinct realms begins to collapse as the service economy develops, as married women move into paid employment, and as in the framework of the women's movement there develops an emancipatory theology of women's rights and liberation. We see this theology as derivative not only from changes in the economy, but also as derivative from other social movements driven by other purposes, and, in turn, pushing changes in the political and economic frameworks of action. The women's movement follows these changes as well as leading it. Thus purposes create interests as well as interests driving purposes.

The movements for women's rights and for women's liberation confront a new reality, and in turn become socially redefined. If growth is limited, and if the positive role of the State *vis-à-vis* women's claims is also limited, women are bargaining in the family, in the world of work, and in the welfare system but with less room for manoeuvre in this new political economic reality. This reduced ability to claim leads to frustration. The State is unable to develop a coherent policy as to whether to encourage women to work or to remain at home. Efforts to achieve equal pay for women run against the occupational structure; equal pay for work of equal value is a slogan without operational leverage. The women's movement itself becomes divided. In this new reality there is no historically unfolding women's interest, but rather alternative ways to move, each holding its own problems, and each affecting differentially different groups of women. We now see the three realms as unified, but in such a way that changes in one realm may as well undercut, as support, changes in another.

This third stage appears as one in which economics takes the centre of the stage; it is described as one in which economic growth has slowed down. It might be believed that we have reached the limit of claiming. But in our view, there is no reason to believe that this stubborn constraint has been reached. Rather, we see this third model as a new social construction of the natural in the service of the current organization of interests and purposes.

NOTES

[1] Gary Becker, 'Economic Analysis and Human Behavior', In *Sociological Economics*, (ed.) Louis Levy-Garboua, Beverly Hills: Sage Publications, 1979, p. 10.
[2] Talcott Parsons, *The Social System*, New York: Free Press of Glencoe, 1951.

Index

Abortion 90, 91, 113-14, 116
Albers, J. 120
American Telephone and Telegraph Company 13, 84, 106
Anthony, Susan 80
Apps, P. 118
Artificial realm 8, 11, 34-5
  intervention 3-4, 7, 13
  see also natural
Australia 12, 68

Bell Telephone Company 77-8
Bentham, J. 7

Caplow, T. 41, 43, 44, 46
Castro, F. 32
Children 22-3, 47-8
China 33
Civil Rights Act (1964) 94, 104
Claims:
  of blacks 107-8
  around capital 24
  conflicts of 29-30, 32-3, 77, 116
  and economic resources 33-4
  within families 22-3, 26-8, 60-1, 71
  formation of 28-9
  interdependencies between 29-30
  package of 20-2
  political claims 32
  process of claiming 102-24
  systems of 22-35, 102-5, 123
  theory of 1-2, 14, 16-35, 133-5
  see also women's claims
Contraception 113-14
Cuba 4, 33, 39

Danziger, S. 82

Economic Opportunity Act (1964) 93
Economic realm 7-9, 11
  claims within 23-4, 26-8, 62
  delineation of 16-19
  intervention within 12
Equal Employment Opportunity Commission 13, 75, 77, 94, 104, 105-6

Equal Pay Act (1963) 104
European Community Survey 66

Family 13-14, 71
  income of 67-70
  nuclear family 73
  as unit of production 10
  see also claims *and* women's claims
Feminism:
  'art' and 'craft' 119-20
  and development economics 119
  and morality 120-1
  redefinition of politics 118
  and religion 121-2
Firestone, S. 112
Fraser, D. 119
Freeman, J. 94, 103, 112
Friedan, B. 111

Gilligan, C. 120
Government:
  domain for claims 24-6, 29-30, 91
  as employer 25, 91-7
  as provider 81-6, 97
  as regulator 86-91
  social role 25
  and women's work 76
Gregory, B. 68

Housework 37-55, 71-3, 118, 119-20
  components of 46-9
  economic value 38
  Marxist analysis 51, 118
  New Home Economics 51
  strategies for change 53-5
  technology of 39-40
  wages for 26, 43, 54
  working hours 39-41

Incentives 30-2, 33, 86
Income distribution 9, 30-2
Industrial society:
  economic analysis of 16-19
  institutional analysis of 18-20
Italy 44

Index

Job structure 9

Knight, F. 18
Kohlberg, L. 121
Kristol, I. 32

Lenin 111

Marginal productivity of wages 31
Mott, Lucretia 108

National Organization for Women 105, 106, 110
Natural:
   and artificial 1-5, 7, 8, 9, 14
   barrier of 1, 74-8
   idea of 1-14, 64, 112, 119, 123-4, 134-5
   and intervention 8
   invention of 6-7
   redefinition 77
   two realms of 7-9, 10, 11, 14

Oakley, A. 41, 43

Parsons, T. 13, 45, 46, 134
Pizzorno, A. 28
Polanyi, K. 16-17, 20
Poverty, views of 5-9
   Malthusian analysis 6

Rainwater, L. 70
Reagan, R. 89
Reich, C. 21
Rein, M. 70

Secondary workers 17-18
Sen, A. 24
Seneca Falls Convention 108
Sex 72
Sex discrimination 105-6
Social realm 7-9, 13
   see also family
Social welfare labour market 95-8
State:
   claims against 21, 26-8
   role of 80-1, 127-9, 130, 132
   social policies 63
   see also government
Stanton, Elizabeth Cady 108
Stretton, H. 118
Sweden 62

Tawney, R. H. 32

Three models of society 127-9
   claiming perspective on 133-5
   Marxist perspective on 131-3
   neo-classical perspective on 129-31, 133
Thurow, L. 94-5

Welfare state 7
   and family 8
Woman suffrage 98, 114, 117
Women, views of 9-14
Women and the State 80-99, 127-9
   within contributory system 82-5
   government employment 92-7
   and needs programmes 86
Women and work 10-11, 13, 24, 59-78
   and educational achievement 70
   government employment 92-7
   and husband's earnings 69-71
   labour-force attachment 63-7, 73-4
   labour-force participation 11, 59-60, 61-2, 63, 65-6, 69, 70, 71, 92
   legal profession 109-10
   in nineteenth century 10
   occupational structure 75-6, 84
   in wartime 3
   working mothers 61-2
   see also housework *and* women's wages
Women's claims 37, 75, 85, 122, 134-5
   in administrative realm 88-90
   in courts 90-1
   within families 41-3, 53, 62, 71-2, 75, 77, 127-9
   interaction between family and work claims 69-74, 113
   in legislative arena 87-8
   within natural 75
   against State 83-4, 99, 127-9
   'theory of two revolutions' 62-3, 71, 74-5
   at work 60-3, 66, 71, 75, 77, 127-9
   see also women's movement
Women's movement 77, 88, 102-24, 130, 134-5
   'women's rights' 109, 115, 124, 134
Women's role within family 1, 13, 45, 60-1, 71-3
   sole head of family 69

Women's wages 12, 94-5
   low wages 74, 76, 83, 85
Wootton, B. 23-4

Zaretsky, E. 10, 44-5, 46, 75
Zetkin, C. 111